Railways of the Raj

Railways of the Raj

MICHAEL SATOW & RAY DESMOND

with a foreword by Paul Theroux

New York University Press · New York *and* London

First published 1980 in the U.S.A. by New York University Press,
Washington Square, New York, N.Y. 10003

Text copyright © Michael Satow and Ray Desmond, 1980

Foreword copyright © Paul Theroux, 1980

Library of Congress Catalog Card Number: 80-82511

ISBN 0-8147-7816-x

The authors would like to acknowledge the help of B. C. Ganguly, B. S. D. Baliga, M. M.
Bery, G. P. Warrier, K. S. Rajan, M. Menezes (Chairmen of the Indian Railways Board,
1969–79); S. M. Chakravarty, M. S. D. Jetley, Ram Kumar (Curators of the Rail
Transport Museum, Delhi, 1969–78); Sir Peter Allen; L. G. Marshall; Colonel M. C.
Perceval-Price; the Embassy of Pakistan; the staff of the Rail Transport Museum, Delhi,
of the Indian Railways, and of the India Office Library and Records. Innumerable
friends in India and Britain have given assistance, but especial thanks are due to Hugh
Hughes for his detailed and painstaking correction of parts of the text.

A large number of the illustrations in this book are reproduced by permission of the
Director of the India Office Library and Records, whence they were obtained. Some
subjects, however, have other sources and the Publishers gratefully acknowledge the help
of the following in giving access to their records, supplying photographs, and granting
permission for material in their possession to be reproduced: Mrs D. Everett (page 31);
James Finlay & Co. (30); Guildhall Library (12, 14–17, 22–3, 44, left-hand plate on 48, 49,
53, 55, 115); Indian Railways Board (34–5, 45, 62, 66, 71–4, 82, 84, 87, 93–4, 97–100,
104–6, 108, 110–11, 116, 118); Foy Nissen (42); Embassy of Pakistan (86); M. G. Satow
(28, 41, 47, 77–80, 103, 107); Paul Theroux (20); Victoria and Albert Museum (38–9).

Printed in Great Britain by Shenval Press, London and Harlow

Frontispiece
The Great India Peninsula Railway terminus and administrative offices at Bombay, now
known as Victoria Terminus. Watercolour by Axel Herman Haig 1878.

Contents

Foreword

The Raj had no shortage of symbols, but the railway was the greatest of them (even today that spinning wheel on India's flag could be the wheel of a locomotive and mean as much). It was the imperial vision on a grand scale; it tested the ideas and inventions of engineers. India was the proving ground for the Victorian imagination: the railway builders sewed together the entire sub-continent with a stitching of track.

It was self-serving, of course; it was, from the beginning, a commercial enterprise, and after the Mutiny the railway with its fortified stations and tunnels was part of the military might of the Raj – the long march and the relief column were supplanted by the troop train. But it had a humane side. It was not, as in East Africa, only an expedient for moving minerals and farm produce to market. The railway was the bloodstream of the Raj, and it affected nearly everyone. It linked the centres of population; and the cities, which until then had been identified with their temples and forts, became identified with their railway stations, Howrah with Calcutta, Victoria with Bombay, Egmore and Madras Central with Madras. It involved millions of people, it required immense paperwork, the clipboard, the manifests in triplicate, the endless chain-of-command from Director to Sweeper – so it suited the complexity of Indian life, and it was an institution of limitless subtlety. Aesthetically, it was pleasing.

Very quickly, the railway became part of Indian legend and a source of romance. Here is an opening paragraph from one of the greatest tales of the Raj:

The beginning of everything was in a railway train upon the road to Mhow from Ajmir. There had been a deficit in the Budget, which necessitated travelling, not Second-class, which is only half as dear as First-class, but by Intermediate, which is very awful indeed. There are no cushions in the Intermediate class, and the population are either Inter-mediate, which is Eurasian, or native, which for a long night journey is nasty, or Loafer, which is amusing though intoxicated. Intermediates do not patronize refreshment-rooms. They carry their food in bundles and pots, and buy sweets from the native sweetmeat-sellers, and drink the roadside water. That is why in the hot weather Intermediates are taken out of the carriages dead, and in all weathers are most properly looked down upon.

This is vintage Kipling, in 'The Man Who Would Be King', and it is interesting not merely because it describes the conditions in which the narrator is about to meet two men who will conquer Kafiristan, but because its seedy effects were patiently collected a year before on the railway in the Rajput states of the Indian desert. And when it was printed in 1888, it appeared as the fifth volume in Wheeler's Railway Series. These pamphlet-sized books with line drawings on their covers were sold at railway bookstalls all over the Raj. This adventure story, researched on a railway, describing a fateful railway journey, and sold on railway platforms, helped to make Kipling's reputation and create the first Kipling boom. Where, one wonders, would Kipling have been without the train?

Eight years after Rudyard Kipling toured the dusty provinces with his notebook on his lap, avowedly in search of material for stories for *The Week's News* and the *Pioneer Mail*, another traveller boarded the Raj railways and, characteristically, introduced a note of comedy. This was Sam Clemens, looking for something to fill Mark Twain's cracker barrel. He had had a success with *Innocents Abroad* and *Roughing It*; he was between books, and he needed money to go on financing the development of the typesetting machine which very nearly bankrupted him. He had also started a publishing company. He needed a selling title. His idea was to circle the globe, giving lectures on the way, and to write a book about it. The book became *Following the Equator*, a bright sprawling travelogue of Hawaii, South Africa, Australia, Ceylon and India. It is very funny, casually learned, and extremely intrepid. It is hard to say why this book has never been reissued. But there is nothing in it for the English Department, no fodder for the graduate student; perhaps that is the reason.

The book you have in your hand offers the report of one traveller who says, 'Every train (except mails) stops at every station a quarter of an hour for purposes of gossip, and at all large stations half an hour or an hour.' Sam Clemens, on various branch lines from Calcutta to Lucknow, wrote about this peculiarly neighbourly use of the railway, but typically he was more expansive.

This train stopped at every village; for no purpose connected with business apparently. We put out nothing, we took nothing aboard. The train hands stepped ashore and gossiped with friends a quarter of an hour, then pulled out and repeated this at succeeding villages. We had thirty-five miles to go and six hours to do it in, but it was plain that we were not going to make it. It was then that the English officers said it was now neces-

sary to turn this gravel train into an express. So they gave the engine driver a rupee and told him to fly. It was a simple remedy. After that we made ninety miles an hour.

He was full of praise for Indian railways, and he was impressed by the fact that they were exclusively manned by Indians of an especially solicitous nature. One day, on his way to Allahabad, he got down at a platform and was so transfixed by the whirl of activity on the platform ('that perenially ravishing show') he did not notice the train starting. But an Indian with a green flag in his hand saw him about to sit down to wait for another train; he approached the American.

'Don't you belong in the train, sir?'
'Yes,' I said.
He waved his flag and the train came back! And he put me aboard with as much ceremony as if I had been the General Superintendent.

Nothing escaped Mr Clemens' notice as he travelled throughout India on the trains, and it was clear to him that the Indians had made the railways their own. They had a knack for inhabiting the stations, washing and sleeping on the platforms, cooking near the shunting engines, arriving days early for a journey and setting up camp in the booking hall. He devotes pages to the crowds and he describes how Hindu caste and railway class produce excruciating ironies: 'Yes, a Brahmin who didn't own a rupee and couldn't borrow one, might have to touch elbows with a rich hereditary lord of inferior caste, inheritor of an ancient title a couple of yards long, and he would just have to stand for it; for if either of the two was allowed to go in the cars where the sacred white people were, it probably wouldn't be the august poor Brahmin.' As for the carriages, 'No car in any country is quite equal its for comfort (and privacy) I think.' Best of all, he said, the most notable feature on the railways of the Raj was their 'cosiness'.

Once they were established, the railways of India blended with the country; they seemed as ancient and everlasting, and the stations as grand and as foolish-seeming and marvellously vain as any maharajah's palace. In South America and in Africa, you look at the railway and see how it has been imposed on the landscape: it sticks out, it doesn't belong, it is a rusty, linear interruption of snoozing greenery, and where are the passengers?

But in India the railway seems to have grown out of the culture, accommodating everyone and everything. There were no obstacles that were not surmounted – the widest river was bridged, the steepest mountainside climbed, the harshest desert crossed. The railway possessed India and made her hugeness graspable. Now, any Bengali with the fare could make his *yatra* from Calcutta to the Kali shrine in distant Simla, the pilgrim could visit the holy hamlet of Rameswaram at the tip of India's nose. The trader could trade, the salesman could sell, and workers on the railway soon numbered in the millions. Indians were no longer marooned by work: they could go home.

There is a seclusion about railway carriages. For an English civil servant who suffered an intense conspicuousness in his post, this seclusion was a relief. We have the word of George Orwell on this. In an unlikely place for such a reminiscence, *The Road to Wigan Pier*, he says,

I remember a night I spent on the train with a man in the Educational Service, a stranger to myself whose name I never discovered. It was too hot to sleep and we spent the night in talking. Half an hour's cautious questioning decided each of us that the other was "safe"; and then for hours, while the train jolted slowly through the pitch-black night, sitting up in our bunks with bottles of beer handy, we damned the British Empire – damned it from the inside, intelligently and intimately. It did us both good. But we had been speaking forbidden things, and in the haggard morning light when the train crawled into Mandalay, we parted as guiltily as any adulterous couple.

It is hard to imagine this episode taking place anywhere but in a railway carriage. It is ironic, though, too. Orwell (who was a policeman at the time) and the stranger did not realise that if it had not been for the Empire they would not have had the safe solitude of the railway in which to damn it.

The railway had few detractors, and it has endured – not as a feeble relic, but as a vital institution. Indeed, it has grown. India is still building locomotives and coaches, and extending the lines.

Today, the flavour of the Raj is less in the rolling-stock than in the timetables, with their complex rules and prohibitions and their curious locutions. Under its twenty-one 'Rules for Passengers', Pakistan Western Railway includes 'Awakening Passengers at Night', 'Ladies Travelling Alone at Night', 'Servants' Tickets' and 'Servants in sole charge of children'. *Notes for the Guidance of Public* describes in detail the uniforms of the catering staff ('Refreshment-room contractors: Plain white chapkan and white pyjamas, with green kamarband, 4″ wide, green turban band 2″ wide and badges' – and so on, six uniforms). There are pages of 'Catering Arrangements' in today's Indian Railway timetable, and these too have that formal exhaustiveness one associates with the Raj, together with some of the Victorian phraseology: 'On prior intimation Chota hazari and evening tiffin will be served in trains at stations where Vegetarian Refreshment Rooms are working. . .'

In an important sense, the Railways of the Raj still exist. The great viaduct still spans the Gokteik Gorge in Upper Burma, Victoria Terminus has not been pulled down to make room for a dual-carriageway, the train from Kalka is still the best way to Simla, and there are steam locomotives huffing and puffing all over India. This artifact of the past is carrying India into the future. I have had the luck to travel the subcontinent on these same rails. 'With typical Victorian loyalty', the authors remark, 'streets were named according to the custom of the age: Church Road, King's Road, Queen's Road . . . Steam Road . . .' I was once in Lucknow and was talking idly with an Indian man. Where did he live? I asked. 'Just down the road', he said, 'in Railway Bazaar.' I made a note of that, and I remember thinking what a marvellous title that would make for a travel book.

Paul Theroux, February 1980

7

Attock ●

Kandahar ●
Chaman
Khojak Tunnel
Quetta
Bolan Pass

Amritsar ●
Simla
Kalka
Ambala

Darjeeling
Siliguri

Delhi

Sukkur

Jodhpur
Jaipur
Agra
Gwalior

Lucknow

Patna
Jamalpur
Arrah
Kiul
Dehri-on-Sone

Karachi

Kota

Allahabad

Raneegunge

Ahmadabad

Bhopal
Jabalpur

Howrah
Calcutta
Kharagpur

Junagad
Baroda

Itarsi

Nagpur

Thull Ghat
Bombay   Thana
Matheran   *Bhore Ghat*
Poona

Hyderabad ●

Bangalore
Mysore
Madras

Ootacumund
Mettupalaiyam
Cochin

0   km   1000

Map of the Indian sub-continent showing places and railway lines to which reference is made in the text.

Pioneers and pioneering

In the year 1600 Queen Elizabeth granted a charter to the London East India Company under the title of 'The Governor and Company of Merchants of London trading into the East Indies'. During the next two hundred years seven subsequent charters were granted, the Company became known as 'The Honourable East India Company' (or less explicitly, the Honourable John Company) and a patchwork government of the land, based on the Presidencies of Bengal, Bombay and Madras, was established. However, the subsequent half-century saw a progressive weakening of its authority and a growth of unrest in the northern provinces culminating in the Great Mutiny of 1857 and the establishment of imperial rule a year later.

It was during the troubled decline of the East India Company that the very British invention, the steam railway, gained its first foothold on Indian soil. While the East India Company was busy developing its trade with India, Britain was equally busy promoting the tide of the Industrial Revolution. The steam engine had unlocked the door to industrial production, but the transport of minerals, raw materials and finished goods was still limited to the power and speed of animals. In 1804 a Cornishman, Richard Trevithick, successfully applied his high pressure steam engine to the propulsion of a wheeled vehicle and the steam locomotive was born. Twenty years later, the efforts and experiments of Blenkinsop, Hedley and Stephenson had developed it to the point of commercial application, and by 1830 the Liverpool and Manchester Railway had set the pattern for land transport for the next hundred years all over the world.

The problems which led to the development of railways in Britain were to be found in one form or another in any land where trade was being developed; India was no exception. Sea traffic was already well developed, but the ports of India were the terminals and beyond them, into the rich hinterland, animal and human power was still the limiting factor. Land transport was disorganised; the roads were unmade and virtually impassable during monsoon periods and the economic range of the bullock cart was fifty miles. The rich coal deposits of Western Bengal and Bihar were expensively remote from Calcutta and supplies of cotton, jute and seeds equally so from Surat, Bombay and Madras where factories tended to concentrate.

The successful establishment of railways in Britain soon led the promoters to seek wider fields for promotion in Europe and further afield. They were quick to enlist the support of other commercial interests and strong lobbies developed in London to persuade, amongst others, the East India Company and the Steam Navigation Company (later to become The Peninsula and Oriental Steam Navigation Company) that they would benefit from the introduction of railways into India. The East India Company would have rapid and cheap access to the potential sources of raw cotton, jute and seeds for their central mills and would be able to move coal quickly and cheaply to the ports, or to new inland factories. Shipping interests would have access to new coal bunkering facilities, particularly in Calcutta. As a bonus, the movement of troops to areas of unrest at short notice could result in more effective deployment of existing garrison forces and would be of interest to the government.

Seen in retrospect the case was overwhelming, but, from the time when the first serious proposals were discussed in 1843, ten years were to pass before the official opening of the first section of the Great Indian Peninsula Railway (G.I.P.R.) over a twenty mile length of track from Bombay to Thana. Had five years of that time been saved, the Indian Mutiny might not have lasted as long as it did or resulted in such bloodshed.

It may seem surprising that six years of argument should have preceded the ultimate approval of the first schemes, but even in the land of their birth there were many detractors. One can imagine the opportunities which were open to them when they were holding forth in London about a situation of which they knew little or nothing, in a territory which neither they nor their audience had visited! India was not a unified country; the proponents of various schemes were based in Bengal, Bombay, Madras and, for strategic rather than commercial reasons, on the North West Frontier. Would the railways attract sufficient freight or passenger traffic to justify the investment and provide an adequate return to the investors; would the natives change their style of living and take to long-distance travel; would they be capable of building, let alone operating and maintaining, the railways? Would the railways be destroyed by the first floods; would termites destroy the wooden sleepers as fast as they were laid? Would trains be blown off the track by storms? The list was endless, but the main stumbling-block to progress remained the question of return on investment.

By 1845, the embryo East Indian Railway Company (E.I.R.) was putting proposals to the Court of the East India Company that the latter should guarantee a minimum return of 3 per cent on investor's capital; a figure which they were subsequently successful in raising to 5 per cent. But it was a long and hard fight. Ranged in favour of the E.I.R. were the railway promoters, commercial interests, banks, shipping and government of the land; against were the rival promoters and other vested interests, with the Court of Directors of the East India Company torn between the acceptance of financial risk or loss of support when its charter was due for renewal in 1853. There was plenty of ammunition supplied by the supporters of both teams. Lord Hardinge, the Governor-General, wrote from Simla in July 1846:

I am confident, however, that the English capitalists will not, without more information on these points (cost of construction and probable profit) and more substantial encouragement from the East India Company, enter into the speculation . . . In this country, where no man can tell one week what the next may produce, the facility of rapid concentration of infantry, artillery and stores may be the chief prevention of an insurrection, the speedy termination of war or safety of the Empire . . .

By October 1846, a confused Court of Directors of the East India Company was faced by the promoters of no fewer than fifteen schemes for railways: six emanating from Calcutta, three from Bombay, four from Madras and two in the Upper Provinces from Allahabad to Delhi and then on to Meerut and Ludhiana. The Governor-General's views were explicit and they had before them the report of the expert committee headed by a railway engineer, F. W. Simms, who had been despatched to India in 1845 to study the situation and prepare recommendations.

Finally, on 17 August 1849 the East India Company signed agreements for two experimental lines, one from Calcutta to Raneegunge (120 miles) and the other from Bombay to Kalyan (30 miles). These lines were to be promoted by the East Indian Railway Company and the Great Indian Peninsula Railway Company respectively. Throughout this period of negotiation it was the East Indian Railway, under the stimulating leadership of Rowland Macdonald Stephenson, which set the pace and finally negotiated terms which were calculated to attract investors. Significant amongst these were the clauses that the East India Company agreed 'to a guarantee of 5 per cent interest on all sums paid with their permission into the Treasury as long as the Railway Company continued to possess the Railway'; and 'all losses in working the railway line to be borne by the Railway Company, but the Railway Company having the liberty to hand over the Railways to the East India Company after giving six months notice, obtaining repayment of the actual capital spent on the construction of the lines, rolling stock etc.'

The East Indian Railway promoters, backed by strong Liberal lobbies in England, had driven a hard bargain and had set the pattern for others to follow. The first round was over. Two experimental railways were to be built with limited capital and if these proved workable and successful, then doubtless the rest would follow. But the co-ordinated network uniting the country and serving strategic needs was still many years away.

Part of the agreement with the railway companies included the provision of free land for the lines and installations by the Government of India on a ninety-nine year lease. It was early in 1851 that land became available to the E.I.R. for construction purposes. The intervening year had been taken up with more arguments about the route and form of the railway out of Calcutta. These discussions might well have dragged on for years because the East India Company and the government had retained considerable powers of control over the railway companies and had established a cumbrous system for exercising it. In effect, the engineer for the railway was responsible for all design work, which then had to be approved by the consulting engineer appointed by the government. If they agreed, work could proceed; if not, the matter had to be referred to the Government of India and, if it could not resolve the problem, it was referred to the supreme government in London. It was a game for any number of players. Additionally, all major policy decisions had to be referred to the government and these included the precise siting of wayside stations!

Two people deserve credit for bringing some order to the scene. One was Colonel J. P. Kennedy, the other was Lord Dalhousie.

Colonel Kennedy was appointed consulting engineer for railways by the Government of India during 1850-1 and in that time he prepared policy guidelines and rules for the construction of the lines. These included the basis for the selection of routes, keeping in mind the need to develop a comprehensive and interconnected network linking centres of population and industry with the ports, and defining gradient limits and the maximum permitted cost/mile of construction (£5,000/mile of single track). He also ruled that all railways should be built as single lines with land and masonry work to provide for subsequent doubling.

Lord Dalhousie was appointed Governor-General of India in 1847 prior to which he had held office as President of the Board of Trade in Britain, an office which had brought him into close contact with the development of railways there. By the time Dalhousie arrived in India, the British railway scene was the subject of what came to be known as 'the battle of the gauges'. George Stephenson had inherited a gauge of 4ft 8in, a dimension probably based on the early rut-ways and owing its origin to the distance between the wheels of a horse-drawn vehicle. This gauge was used for the building of the Stockton and Darlington Railway (1825) and subsequently (increased to 4ft 8½in for technical reasons) for the Liverpool and Manchester Railway (1830). When Brunel engineered the Great Western Railway (1838), his expansive mind broke with tradition and he adopted the broad gauge of 7ft 0in on the grounds that it would provide stability and steadier running at high speeds.

Dalhousie was well aware of the growing battle in England and was equally aware of the folly of having more than one gauge in a national railway system. Under the circumstances likely to prevail in India, he favoured a broad gauge rather than the 4ft 8½in which had been advocated or assumed in the formative discussions of the 1840s and expressed his personal preference for 6ft 0in. The final compromise turned out to be 5ft 6in on the grounds of economy of capital and the fact that other railways had already adopted this gauge. This agreed, Dalhousie then decreed that it be adopted as the standard for all lines built or proposed in India. In his words: 'The British Legislature fell into the mischievous error of permitting the introduction of two gauges in the United Kingdom . . . The Government of India has in its power, and no doubt will carefully provide that, however widely the railway system may be extended in this Empire in the time to come these great evils should be averted . . .' It was to be a mere nineteen years before the resolve weakened and the grand plan was abandoned.

Sir James Andrew Broun Ramsay, first Marquess and tenth Earl of Dalhousie, (1812–60). Governor-General of India 1847–56.

There were many other problems to engage Dalhousie's attention over the building of the first line out of Calcutta. The East Indian Railway had available just under £1 million of capital with which to establish an experimental line which was to be laid, on the instructions of the East India Company, with double track. Simms' calculations showed that this sum of money would be adequate for ninety-two miles of double track, so that it would effectively terminate in 'no man's land' and, more importantly, some thirty miles short of the coal fields at Raneegunge which were to be its life blood. The need for Dalhousie to have to make what must have seemed the elementary decision to lay a single track all the way to Raneegunge must have taxed his self-restraint to the limit. In an ensuing paragraph he wrote:

Lastly, if the experimental section be constructed in literal conformity with the orders of the Court, of a double line and only so as not to compromise the Government in the slightest degree . . . I conceive that this section, commercially, must be a total failure. If the object . . . is to prove the practicability of forming a railway as a public work, the fact could be proved on a quarter of the distance and at a quarter of the expenses. If, as I have assumed, the object in view is to prove the profitableness as well as the practicability of a railway in India, I regard this proposal as totally useless. The Government might as well construct a railway from the Gaol to the General Hospital.

The first section of the East Indian Railway was officially opened

Byculla Station, on the Bombay-Tanna (Thana) line in 1854. Note the single wire telegraph line in the background. (*Illustrated London News*, 2 September 1854.)

to traffic on 15 August 1854 and it reached Raneegunge on 3 February 1855 by a single track of 5ft 6in gauge.

Whilst the East Indian Railway was sorting out its early problems with Dalhousie's help, the Great Indian Peninsula Railway was making rather more rapid progress. Once Dalhousie had settled the gauge problem it was a question of building the line, initially to Thana (twenty miles) and then across the Thana creek by a bridge of twenty-two stone arches and on to Kalyan (ten miles from Thana). The inaugural train set out from Bombay (Bori Bunder) on 16 April 1853 (some five months after the line was completed) and the creek was bridged and the line through to Kalyan thirteen months later. The 'English Machine' had arrived, heralded, somewhat lyrically, by the *Overland Telegraph and Courier* as

a triumph, to which, in comparison, all our victories in the East seem tame and commonplace. The opening of the Great Indian Peninsula Railway will be remembered by the natives of India when the battlefields of Plassey, Assaye, Meanee and Goojerat have become the landmarks of history.

The official opening of the Bombay-Thana section of the Great Indian Peninsula Railway was doubtless a triumph for the promoters and the engineers, but less so for those who organised the ceremonial of the occasion. For some inexplicable reason, Lord Falkland, Governor of Bombay, and a number of other important personages departed for the hills a matter of hours before the ceremony. Public opinion, as expressed by the *Bombay Times* was critical:

The Governor, Lord Falkland and the Commander-in-Chief, Lord Frederick Fitz-Clarence, with their respective attendants accompanied by the Bishop, The Reverend John Hardinge, left for the hills the evening previous in disregard of the memorable character of the occasion.

No reason seems to have been recorded for this rebuff; an act which seems even more strange when we read that Lady Falkland witnessed the occasion. But in spite of what appears to have been an official rebuff, the occasion seems to have been enjoyed by those who stayed behind. The day was declared a public holiday; the Governor's band provided the musical accompaniment, and at 3.30pm a train loaded with 400 passengers left Bombay, Bori Bunder station, to the cheers of the multitude and a salute from twenty-one guns. Toasts were drunk to the success of the Company and congratulations were bestowed upon the Chief Engineer, Mr J. J. Berkeley.

With the first section open to traffic, attention was turned to the task of completing the line to Kalyan. This section involved the bridging of the Thana Creek and the driving of two tunnels, but it was ready for opening on 1 May 1854. This time the ceremonial seems to have been more successful, and was performed by the Governor, then Lord Elphinstone. Public opinion must have been one of wonderment, tinged with awe for

Thousands upon thousands came to see that wonder of wonders. The whistle of the engine as it dashed on its glorious course was thought to be the voice of the demon.

On the other side of the continent, the East Indian Railway was facing further problems. The ship carrying the pattern carriages, which may in this case have been models, sank when entering the Hooghly river and there was some delay in shipping out the first locomotives. One account refers to the locomotives having been inadvertently delivered to Australia, but it seems more likely that the small barque *Kedgeree* (686 tons only) took refuge in Western Australia during a storm, for her voyage took four months instead of the usual three. Nearer Calcutta, a dispute arose over the location of the boundary of Chandernagar, a parcel of French territory some twenty-five miles along the line from Howrah (Calcutta). If the boundary was where the French claimed it to be, the line was encroaching on their territory and much time was lost in settling this international dispute. However, Mr John Hodgson, the railway's Locomotive Chief Engineer, was a man of resource and set about designing his own carriages which were built by two coachbuilding firms in Calcutta, Seton & Company and Steward & Company. The locomotives eventually arrived on 3 May 1854, and on 28 June one of them made a trial trip as far as Pundooah. In spite of these efforts, it was not until 3 February 1855 that the line was opened throughout to Raneegunge, the ceremony being performed, appropriately, by Lord Dalhousie. Unfortunately, His Lordship was unwell and was unable to join the passengers in the inaugural train when it left Howrah.

Howrah station is now one of the largest in Asia. At the time of the official opening in 1855, it was little more than a jumble of huts, sheds and stores in the midst of a small village which could only be reached from Calcutta by ferry boats across the Hooghly. Many years later a floating pontoon bridge was constructed, but this had to be opened frequently to allow the passage of shipping, and passengers had to endure delays and confusion when approaching the station. It was nearly ninety years before a high-level bridge was constructed, but even this has far from cured the congestion which attends the station approaches.

Meanwhile, in the south, the Madras Railway was following on with its first experimental line. This was laid between Veyasarpandy (Madras) and Walajah Road (Arcot) and formed the first (sixty-three mile) section which eventually joined Madras and the west coast. The first section was opened on 1 July 1856 and, by then, three experimental lines were in operation. Traffic returns equalled or exceeded expectation and sights were already on the ultimate goal of a network of railways linking the ports with the centres of commerce, and serving the strategic needs of the government. But there was unease in the land, the East India Company had little more than a year to live, and the advantages of railways for moving troops and stores loomed large in the minds of the keepers of the peace.

The War of Independence, or the Great Mutiny, according to which side was reporting events, erupted in May 1857 at Meerut, some thirty miles north of Delhi, and spread rapidly through the line of country south and east towards Calcutta along the route planned for the East Indian Railway. At the time of the outbreak, the line from Calcutta to Delhi was either being surveyed or constructed, according to the progress made on various intermediate sections. Between Allahabad and Cawnpore and between Agra and Delhi, construction was under way and the first forty-four miles from Allahabad were placed at the disposal of the government for the movement of troops and supplies. Considerable damage was done to rail-

way works; progress was halted and railway engineers, frequently in isolated communities, were forced to take refuge or defend themselves and their families as best they could. Many lost their lives, but those who were able to escape joined volunteer forces and assisted with the establishment of fortifications and defences and with the movement of troops and supplies; tasks for which their training and experience fitted them well. Hodgson, the first Locomotive Chief Engineer of the East Indian Railway, died of cholera on 20 June 1857, but his successor, Lingard Stokes, prepared designs for locomotives to be fitted into river barges with paddles driven by the driving wheels of the locomotive. These were used by the government for transport during the mutiny and, later, by the railway for moving materials to construction depots when work was resumed.

In one instance, a group of railway engineers and contractors retreated in the face of a violent mob and took refuge in the newly-built overhead water tank for supplying water to locomotives; a desperate position which they held successfully until rescued by a party sent out from Allahabad to their aid. In another dramatic siege, Richard Vicars Boyle, aged thirty-six, engineer in charge of the section of the line at Arrah, displayed forethought and courage in successfully withstanding, with a handful of colleagues and fifty Sikh police, an attack by some 2,500 sepoys who had mutinied at Dinapore. At that time the railhead was still at Raneegunge and progress of construc-

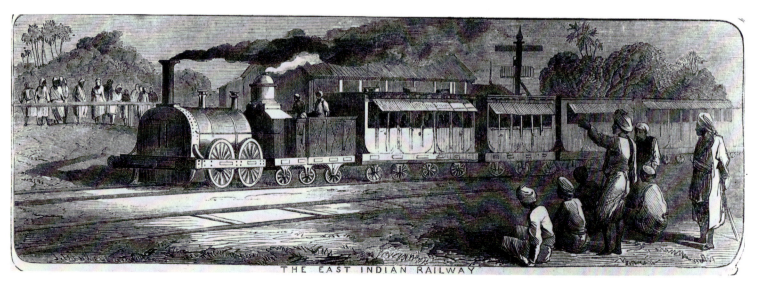

THE EAST INDIAN RAILWAY

The Great Indian Peninsula Railway. The artist, J. Benwell, has separated the engine and tender in front of the firebox. The engine, which has become a 0-4-0, is meant to be one of the original Tayleur 0-4-2 class with four-wheel tender! Note the single post, double arm signal and the early sunshades over the carriage windows. The leading coach with oil lamps in the roof, must be first class; the others, unlit lower class. (*Illustrated London News*, 4 June 1853.)

tion in the sections beyond at Dinapore and Arrah was seriously impeded by unrest amongst local tribes. Boyle sensed a crisis and quietly started to fortify a small building which stood in his garden and served as a billiard room. He bricked up the verandah, laid in emergency provisions and arms and generally made ready to withstand attack. Wives and families had been despatched from Arrah to Dinapore, some twenty-six miles down the line. Mr Herwald Wake, the District Magistrate, had called for and received a detachment of fifty Sikh police in the face of increasing unrest and trouble in the area.

On 25 July, the sepoys at Dinapore mutinied and by the 27th, they had arrived at Arrah, where they released all the prisoners in the jail and looted the treasury. They then concentrated their attention on the 'Little House at Arrah', where Boyle, Wake and fourteen others had taken refuge with the Sikh police. The mutineers brought up two guns, one mounted on the roof of Boyle's residence and commanding the 'Little House' at about sixty yards range, with which they attempted to demolish Boyle's fortress. For seven days, the little group withstood the attack. On 29 July a relief force was ambushed and driven off with heavy casualties, but on 2 August, a second relief, led by Major Vincent Eyre, attacked the mutineers with a force of 160 men of the Fusiliers and twelve volunteers of the railway force. Outnumbered fifteen to twenty times, Eyre successfully turned the flank of the rebel forces, broke them in disorder and relieved the

The 'Little House at Arrah' in the grounds of the bungalow occupied by Richard Vicars Boyle, sketched by Major Vincent Eyre who led the successful relief on 2 August 1857.

Boyle was awarded Rs10,000 per annum for life and decorated with the C.S.I. for his bravery and organisation of the defences. (*Illustrated London News*, 12 December 1857.)

beleaguered inmates of the 'Little House'. Eyre lost two men and fourteen were wounded. Of Boyle's party, one Sikh had been wounded seriously; the rest to only a minor extent. Provisions were all but exhausted, but they were safe. Boyle continued in the service of the railway until 1864 and died at the age of eighty-seven in 1908.

Six months after its outbreak, the Mutiny was effectively quelled and railway construction was again in hand with renewed impetus. Whether the existence of a continuous railway between Calcutta and Meerut in 1857 would have altered the course of Indian history is open to doubt. It might have shortened the agony of the Mutiny, but it is unlikely that the East India Company would have survived much longer. The astrologers had been forecasting that the Raj of the East India Company would end after one hundred years. Ninety-nine years had passed since the battle of Plassey; the stars were in the right conjunction and it would have needed more than a line of rails to divert the course of events.

Much has been made of the Mutiny and its effect on the building of the railways but it was, in effect, merely another of the obstacles to be overcome. It certainly delayed, by some six months, the extension of the East Indian network, but it had little direct effect outside its territory. The building of railways in the west and south proceeded in the face of natural rather than man-made obstacles.

The railways of this period were built by sheer weight of numbers. Skilled teams would be recruited from areas where the skills were traditional (e.g. stonemasons from Rajasthan), but labourers would be recruited from local villages. The news of regular employment, however arduous the work, or however low the wages, would spread like wildfire into the hinterland. Bridges, tunnels and major earthworks demanded high concentrations of labour and a construction force of 10–20,000 was commonplace, with individual camps of 5–10,000. Apart from the Mutiny and the occasional encounter with hostile tribes through whose territory the engineers were surveying

A skirmish in 1856 between engineers of the East Indian Railway and armed Santals in which several engineers were severely wounded. The railway was used for the transport of troops to quell the uprising. (*Illustrated London News*, 9 August 1856.)

and building, it was the health of the construction teams which formed an ever present concern and threat to progress. Dysentery, typhus, cholera and malaria were endemic and, under the primitive conditions of the construction camps, frequently became epidemic. It was not uncommon for a camp of 10,000 to have lost up to one third of its population within a month of an outbreak of cholera. The scourge of sickness was unpredictable, but the climate, with or without the side effects on health, proved another and more regular obstacle to progress. Every hot season brought, if nothing else, the slowing of progress as the shade temperature mounted, to be followed by the monsoon rains during which all progress might be stopped and material damage inflicted on part-finished works. Miles of embankments and thousands of tons of masonry could well disappear in one day when the inexorable force of flood waters was unleashed upon them.

In the face of these common and ever-present enemies, however, the engineers maintained a dogged progress against the natural physical obstacles of the terrain. The East Indian Railway was faced with the seemingly endless flat land of the plains, intersected by the innumerable rivers which dried to a trickle for many months of the year but swelled to flood proportions during the rains, frequently overflowing and breaking their banks and scouring new channels for themselves by the time the flood subsided. The initial policy was to build, as quickly as possible, the sections between these obstacles, relying on ferry services to link the railheads on the river banks. In this manner, and with progressive bridging of the rivers in the ensuing years, the line from Calcutta to Ghaziabad (near Delhi) was completed by 1864 and a year later, Delhi was linked with Multan, on the Indus river (now in Pakistan) by the Punjab and Delhi Railways. The first strategic link was substantially complete.

Meanwhile, the Great Indian Peninsula Railway was faced with an additional problem. In order to link Bombay with the rest of India,

Pioneer of the narrow gauge: the 2ft 6in tramway for the Gaekwar of Baroda between Myagam and Dhaboi. 'His Highness has ordered small engines for this line; but he will probably find animal power better adapted to the traffic, which is exclusively in native passengers and goods. One pair of bullocks will draw five loaded waggons at from two to three miles an hour. The passenger trains may be worked either by country ponies or trotting bullocks.' The three engines (0-4-0ST) proved too heavy for the light track and did not enter regular service until 1873, by which time they had been converted to tender engines to reduce the axle loading. By 1914, the Gaekwa's Baroda State Railways had extended to over three hundred miles of narrow gauge. (*Illustrated London News*, 23 May 1863.)

it had to find routes to the north, east and south. Bombay is an island, or more correctly, an artificial coalescence of islands off the west coast of India. Penetrating beyond the coastal strip of the mainland involved overcoming the natural barrier of the Western Ghats, a formidable and sheer outcrop forming the western ridge of the Deccan Trap, a vast volcanic plug stretching south-east from Bombay towards Bangalore and Madras. This spectacular ridge rises sharply from the coastal strip to a height of some 2,500 feet and routes to Poona and Madras and to Delhi and Calcutta would inevitably involve penetration or ascent of its formation. After much debate and several surveys, two routes were chosen. One, to the north and east, involved a route up and over the Ghats by way of the Thull Ghat and Bhusaval; the other, to the south-east, by way of the Bhore Ghat, to Poona. Of the two the Bhore Ghat proved the more formidable and involved the use of a reversing station where the train, having proceeded up the incline in one direction, had to reverse and continue its climb in the opposite direction (see plate on p. 54). The incline was unremitting and after unsuccessful trials with paired 0-4-0ST engines, banking engines of special design and somewhat ungainly appearance were employed to assist at the rear of the ascending trains. Descending the ghats was equally a problem for the early braking systems were, sadly, not always equal to the task and even with a banking engine added to the head of the train, runaways were not unknown. It is interesting to note that the problem of braking on the long descent worried the superintending engineer when the scheme was in its early stages of planning. One of the possible solutions put forward to safeguard descending trains was an atmospheric system, similar to the ill-fated South Devon line in England. This involved the use of a large tube laid in the ground between and below the rails. A piston in the tube was connected by a vertical bracket to the train above, the tube having a continuous slot to permit the passage of the bracket. This slot was sealed by a leather flap which was lifted by a 'shoe' arrangement to permit the passage of the bracket. Evacuation of the tube ahead of the piston would drive the train forward, evacuation behind the piston would retard it. Stationary lineside pumping engines provided the vacuum. Inevitably, the matter came to Dalhousie's attention and he, whilst admitting to little personal experience, commented: 'with complete deference to opinions better than mine, I must need say that according to existing experience of atmospheric railways this seems to me to be a desperate nostrum.' In the course of its ascent of the ghat, the line had to rise from just above sea level to 2,027 feet. In addition to

the reversing station, there were twenty-five tunnels, totalling 4,000 yards, together with twenty-two bridges. The average workforce was 30–40,000 people and, by the time the work was completed, some 30 per cent had lost their lives through accident or disease.

Amongst the casualties was Solomon Tredwell. He was the contractor engaged to build the line after Faviell of London, the original contractor, had withdrawn. Tredwell arrived in Bombay on 15 September 1855, but whilst visiting the incline he was taken ill and died fifteen days after landing. In one of the epics of railway engineering, it was his widow, Alice Tredwell, who took over. She engaged two of the railway's resident engineers who had worked with Faviell, George H. Clowson and Swanston Adamson, and carried the contract through to completion. The line was finally opened on 14 May 1863. An ex-pupil of Robert Stephenson (the consultant for the work), Mr J. J. Berkeley, was still Chief Engineer for the Railway and is said to have 'praised Mrs Tredwell and Messrs Clowson and Adamson for the manner in which the work was executed'. It certainly rated as one of the major undertakings of its day and Alice Tredwell deserves a place of honour in railway engineering history.

By 1868 the building of the main lines was proceeding apace. The Great Indian Peninsula was almost at Jubbulpore on its way towards the north and Delhi; Nagpur on the eastward route (subsequently half-way house to Calcutta when the Bengal-Nagpur Railway link was completed), and Sholapur, some 150 miles beyond Poona on the south-eastern route towards South India and Madras. The East Indian Railway had established its link from Howrah (Calcutta) to Ghaziabad (near Delhi) and the Madras Railway had completed nearly 200 miles on its way towards the west coast, its link with the Great Indian Peninsula and Bombay.

The year marks what might well be called the end of the first phase. The main trunk lines were progressing in the face of the problems of terrain, climate, sickness and available funds. All the lines were being built to a uniform gauge. Some 4,000 miles were completed and it would be only a matter of time before they were linked and traffic would flow across the length and breadth of the land.

By 1869 the government had hardened its attitude to guarantees for new lines and started to build its own State lines. It was preparing to exercise its option to purchase lines built under the guarantee system after the first twenty-five years of life. '. . . both in raising capital and expenditure that may be required for the new lines in India, the Government should secure for itself the full benefit of the credit which it lends, and of the cheaper agencies at its command' wrote

೪೨

ಒನೇ ಪಾಠ.

ಹೊಗೆ ಯಂತ್ರದ ಚಿತ್ರ.

ರೇಲ್ವೆ ಅಂದರೆ ಕಬ್ಬಿಣ ಭಾಟೆ. ಇದು ಸಮವಾದ ಹಾದಿ
ಯಲ್ಲಿ ದಿಮ್ಮಿಗಳ ಹಾಸಿ ಅದರ ಮೇಲೆ ಕಬ್ಬಿಣದ ಸಲಾ
ಕಿಗಳ ಇರಿಸಿ ಬಿಗಿದು ಮಾಡೋಣಾಗಿ ಇರುತ್ತದೆ. ಈ
ಸಲಾಕಿಗಳ ಮೇಲೆ ಹೊಗೆ ಯಂತ್ರ ಸಾಕಾದ ನೀರಿನ ಹಬೆ
ಯ ಬಲದಿಂದ ಅನೇಕ ಬಂಡಿಗಳ ಸಾಲುಗಳನ್ನು ಎಳಕೊಂ
ಡು ಓಡುತ್ತದೆ. ಇದರ ಓಟ ಬಹು ವೇಗ, ಕುದುರೆಯ
ನಾಗಾಲು ಓಟಕ್ಕಿಂತ ಹೆಚ್ಚಾದಂಥಾದ್ದು. ಇದು ಒಂದು
ಘಂಟೆ ಹೊತ್ತಿಗೆ ೩೦ ಅಥವಾ ೪೦ ಫಳಿಗೆ ದೂರ ಹೋಗುತ್ತದೆ.
ಇದರ ಹಿಂದೆ ತಗಲಿಸುವ ಸಮಾರೀ ಬಂಡಿಗಳಲ್ಲಿ ಪಯಣ
ಹೋದರೆ ವೆಚ್ಚ ಕೂಡಿ ಬರುತ್ತದೆ, ಬಹು ಸಲಕರಣೆಯೂ
ಸಂತೋಷವೂ ಸಹ ಉಂಟು. ಆದ್ದರಿಂದ ಈ ಭಾಟೆ ಎಲ್ಲಿ
ಲ್ಲಿ ಆಗುತ್ತದೋ ಅಲ್ಲಲ್ಲಿ ಜನರೂ ಸಾಮಾನುಗಳೂ ಇದ
ರಲ್ಲಿ ಹೊರ್ತು ಬೇರೆ ಯಾತರಲ್ಲೂ ಹೋಗುವದಿಲ್ಲ.

———.

Extract on railways in the *Cannerese First Book*, published for the government schools by
the Director of Public Instruction at Bangalore in 1868. The reader is told that the engines
have a 'terrific speed, more than the fastest running horse' and that unlike bullock carts
the carriages do not sway from side to side.

the Duke of Argyll, Secretary of State for India in 1869. But the government, having assumed a responsibility for financing and building railways, found itself faced with shortage of funds and cast around for economies. One obvious solution would be to build lighter and narrower gauge lines; thus the gauge question, so clearly resolved by Dalhousie, was reopened under the Viceroy, Lord Lawrence, in 1868. By 1870 the then Viceroy, Lord Mayo, who had plans to introduce the metric system of weights and measures into India, approved the adoption of the metre gauge for the new lines to be built by the State. He summarised his views, somewhat glibly perhaps, when he said: 'When we have an elephant's load, we may use an elephant, but when we have only a donkey's load, we have to use a donkey.' Eighty years later, India was busily adopting the metric system and the railways were embarking on a mammoth programme of conversion from metre to broad gauge. The 'battle of the gauges', which Dalhousie had been at pains to avoid, had started and it only needed an extension of Lord Mayo's philosophy to justify the spread of even narrower gauges. Within ten years the 2ft 6in gauge formed an extensive minor railways network around Baroda, whilst in the hills, the 2ft 0in gauge had been adopted for the Darjeeling-Himalayan Railway because there was no room for anything wider.

In 1880, under Lord Ripon, a modified guarantee system was introduced and the formation of new companies and lines received a fresh impetus. During the next twenty years railway building in India reached its peak, and so by the beginning of the twentieth century India had a network of lines calculated to serve the commercial, social and strategic needs of the land.

Chappar Rift by H. H. Hart, *c.* 1890–5. The Louise Margaret Bridge named after and visited by the Duchess of Connaught at the opening of the Sind Peshin State Railway in 1887. Dwarfed by the rift it spanned, this masterpiece of construction on the North West Frontier survived until the line was breached and abandoned in 1942. In 1944 the girders were recovered for re-use by a feat of engineering which equalled that of its construction. The rails were 233 feet above the bottom of the gorge.

20

Engineers and fire-carriages

It was inevitable that the British dominance of India would result in the adoption of British practice in the building of railways, and in their equipment. The lines themselves and the associated metal-work for bridges, signals and rolling stock had to be imported together with the locomotives, so that the early lines followed closely on established British patterns.

The availability of timber, masonry, bricks (albeit of low quality) and abundant labour provided the basis for the civil engineering and the construction of rolling stock. Considerable experience already existed in the building of major irrigation canals and aqueducts and, much as had happened in Britain two decades earlier, the navigators turned to railway building.

Large bridges were, and continued to be, a major problem. The rivers of northern India are fed mainly by the Himalayan snow and discharge their waters into the Bay of Bengal in the vicinity of Calcutta. In so doing, they traverse hundreds of miles of almost flat land largely composed of the silt which they have deposited over the centuries. The Ganges and the Jamuna have their sources in the Western Himalaya finding their way to the Bay of Bengal by running south through what used to be the Upper Provinces (Uttar Pradesh) past Delhi and then turning eastwards past Lucknow, Benares and Patna and then southwards towards the Bay of Bengal. At this last turn, they are joined by the Brahmaputra which has arrived from the eastern reaches of Assam and between them and their many tributaries they form an incredible and complex system of rivers comprising the Gangetic Delta. The other source of water feeding this vast network is the monsoon rain, falling between the months of June and September each year. During the dry period, the rivers shrink to a sluggish, steady flow in the course of which silt is deposited on the bed. When the monsoon rains come, the flow increases to a flood and, the river bed having been raised by silt during the dry period, the river rises correspondingly with each monsoon. The inevitable happens; the rivers overtop their banks, be they natural or man-made, and find a new route across the flat land. When the floods subside, the river may have abandoned its original route and gouged a new channel. There is no easy solution to the problem. Building higher and stronger banks would merely postpone the day when the flow could no longer be contained and the ensuing disaster would be all the worse.

For a contemporary view of the scene, one cannot do better than quote G. W. MacGeorge in *Ways and Works in India* (Westminster 1894):

The first division of the railway from Howrah to Burdwan, and northward to Rajmahal and the Ganga Valley, traverses a low portion of Deltaic land, subject to extreme inundation ... where the drainage problems to be encountered and solved by the engineers of the railway were of exceptional and extraordinary magnitude. Over this wide expanse of level country, subject to an excessive tropical rainfall, inundations from the flood spill of the enormous channel of the Ganga and other great rivers are often spread as a vast sheet over miles of country, converting the whole district into the semblance of an inland sea from which only the inhabited villages along the higher marginal levels emerge.

Against this background the bridge builders had to find ways of building bridges on ground which might be silt to a depth of a hundred feet or more, keeping them there against the ravages of surging monsoon flows and keeping the river under the bridge in spite of its propensity for changing its course.

The solution to the foundation problem lay in sinking well foundations through the silt until a suitable load-bearing stratum was reached. Usually this involved a depth of 60 to 100 feet, though in extreme cases 140 feet was necessary. Each pier of the bridge was supported on one or more wells which might be 12–20 feet in diameter. The well was formed by constructing a circular timber base with a cutting edge at the bottom and onto this was built a brick wall. When the well reached a height of some 12–20 feet, silt was excavated from inside the well so that it sank into the ground. As the top of the brickwork approached ground level, excavation was stopped and further brickwork was added above, the process being repeated until the desired depth had been reached. In order to assist the sinking operation as the depth and friction increased, it became necessary to add several hundred tons of extra weight to the top – usually using any available rails or girders to hand. When the well had sunk, the ballast had to be removed before the next stage of brickwork could be added, so that the process, elegantly simple in concept and execution, became time-consuming and tedious. One of the main problems was to ensure that the work on well sinking started during the dry season, was in a fit state to withstand the onslaught of the river when swollen by the next rains, for if the rains were early, or delays had occurred in the well-sinking programme, the damage could be enormous. But completion of the wells and their capping was only part of the problem. Nature does not submit easily and rows of wells across a previously unobstructed waterway were an immediate target for her torrents. Heavy scouring caused by the eddies where the water met the upstream side of the well would result in wholesale excavation of the silt to depths of fifty feet or more, leaving the well unsupported so that it would then topple over. There was, in the early days, little experience in dealing with the problem but it was brought under control by dumping large quantities of stone or concrete blocks around the wells. In the meantime, many disasters occurred, experience was hard won and much ingenuity and initiative was displayed in righting canted wells which had all but fallen over.

Once the wells had been sunk and capped, and the piers of masonry or brick had been built, the iron had to be erected. This was almost entirely fabricated in Britain, trial erected, and then dismantled for shipment to an Indian port for transport to the site. Once on site, girders and sections had to be riveted into completed trusses before launching across the respective spans.

Some idea of the scale of these operations can be gained from the Sone river bridge near Arrah on the East Indian Railway. This bridge has a total length of 4,726 feet, made up of 28 decked spans of 157 feet each. Each pier was supported on three brick wells of 18 feet diameter, making a total of 81 wells. For much of the year the bridge spans an endless expanse of dry silt, with only a trickle of water passing below the middle spans, but during the rains it swells to a torrent which drains 23,000 square miles and discharges not far short of two million cubic feet of water per second into the River Ganges near Patna. Construction was started in 1856, was disrupted during the risings of 1857 and was completed in 1863. The opening ceremony was performed by Lord Elgin who paid tribute to the achievement

A touch of Victorian fantasy. Cast-iron pier frames for the Kuil and Harohar bridges on the East Indian Railway to the design of A. M. & G. Rendel. The frames are being assembled at the Woodside Ironworks of Messrs Cochrane and Co., near Dudley in 1858. (*Illustrated London News*, 18 September 1858.)

with the words: 'this magnificent bridge was exceeded in magnitude by only one bridge in the world'. It was indeed a triumph for the pioneer bridge builders in India. Forty years later it was eclipsed by the Upper Sone Bridge of 93 spans totalling 10,052 feet.

The story of bridge building in India is graphically recounted in *Couplings to the Khyber* by P. S. A. Berridge, one-time bridge engineer to the North Western Railway. During these years, when all the iron and steelwork was fabricated in Britain, the bridge engineers became known by their brethren in the offices of the consultants in London and on the railways of Britain as 'the Meccano engineers' since all they had to do was 'screw them together when they arrived'! Little can they have known of the conditions under which the foundations had to be established, or of the hostile terrain in which they had to be erected. History does not relate the comments of the Meccano engineers when called upon to erect such incredible and intractable structures as the Lansdowne Bridge across the Indus River between Sukkur and Rohri.

Most of the bridges built by these pioneers are still in service. With increasing traffic and with doubling of single-track lines, many of them have been strengthened or widened by regirdering. Some incredible feats of organisation and co-ordination were achieved during these operations and it was not uncommon for a complete span to be removed and replaced by a new and heavier one in the space of two to three hours.

The ready availability of good quality timber, Burma teak of the highest quality and Central Provinces teak of lower grade, and the existence of established coachbuilding firms in India led naturally to the construction of railway rolling stock in India from the outset. Designs and specifications were prepared in Britain and it was the practice to make builders' models or full-size pattern coaches to be shipped out to the local firms engaged to make the stock. This technique effectively provided a three-dimensional drawing which did much to overcome the barriers of language and illiteracy which would have attended the interpretation of paper instructions.

These models did not always arrive safely at their intended destination, and on such occasions local initiative took over with results which may well have been no worse and, in some cases, more appropriate to local skills and techniques.

Early coaching and wagon stock was of the four-wheeled variety, following closely on contemporary British practice, but local variations and refinements soon made their appearance as experience was

Trolleying down from the Khojak tunnel to New Chaman. 'There are few more exciting journeys to be made than a trip at full speed on the Inspector's trolley . . . from Sheelabagh . . . through the thick darkness . . . out into the dazzling sunshine . . . the cold mountain air; down the dizzy slopes . . . the shining rails lead through the lower sandhills . . . into the last British outpost at New Chaman.' (*Graphic*, 26 May 1894.)

gained under alien conditions. Inevitably, the lot of the lower class passenger was disproportionately worse than that of the more elevated traveller.

Early designs of rolling stock were conventional in their use of wooden frames and bodies. Nominally, roofs, but not windows, were provided from the outset to give some protection from the tropical sun or monsoon downpours, but lower class passengers frequently found themselves exposed to the elements in reserve stock cobbled together by fitting benches into open wagons when demand exceeded supply of regular stock. This was a frequent and persistent situation, for the Indians, whose propensity for travel by rail was seriously doubted by the early promoters, or their antagonists, soon took to the railways in swarms. Several railways tackled the overcrowding problem in the early 1860s by building double-deck lower class coaches. Doubtless these were better than open wagons, but the lack of headroom meant that the operative word was 'sit'. One minor concession to comfort appeared fairly early, the sunshade and the double roof. Conditions in roofed vehicles in the hot weather, with a relentless sun beating down from overhead could be well nigh intolerable, and it was doubtless local improvisation which led to the fitting of sunshades along the eaves of the vehicles to shade the window openings and the fitting of an outer roof with a space through which air could circulate to cool the inner skin.

In 1874 overcrowding was again solved by removing seats from third-class carriages and designating them fourth class. Not surprisingly this palliative was short-lived; seats were reinstated, fourth became third and third became intermediate below second.

The basic pattern for lower class coaching stock changed little for some thirty years following the introduction of railways to India, until the first wooden-bodied coaches on steel underframes were introduced in 1885.

By 1903, after an interim period of rigid and articulated six-wheelers, bogie stock was displacing the four-wheelers, electric light and fans had made their appearance and the way was open to the production of coaches which could provide standards of comfort comparable with those of European railways. In general bogies and underframes were imported, whilst the bodies were built at the carriage and wagon workshops of the respective railways. The continuous vacuum brake was adopted in 1879 and it is significant that its application to freight wagons was far more rapid than in Britain.

The early locomotives were ordered by competitive tender from Britain and followed closely the existing trends of design and develop-

ment. 2-4-0 and 0-4-2 wheel arrangements, with inside cylinders predominated for passenger and mixed traffic duties. The first engines for the Great Indian Peninsula Railway bore the plates of Vulcan Foundry, and amongst other early suppliers to India were Beyer, Peacock, E. B. Wilson, Stothert and Slaughter, Kitson, Thompson and Hewitson. Apart from the addition of large canopy cabs, the engines were fairly standard proprietary products.

With the adoption of the metre gauge by the Indian State Railways came the first of a range of standard engines which were designed specifically for the State lines and ordered in batches for allocation as needed. These engines continued to feature the 2-4-0 and 0-4-2 wheel arrangements in tender and tank form, but with outside cylinders and, in most cases, outside frames. Valves were between the frames, with the exception of the A-class 2-4-0 tank engines, and were operated by Stephenson or Allan link motion. This range of engines, being of standard design, was also ordered by competitive tender and from this time on, we find the list of suppliers spreading rapidly amongst the British locomotive builders. These were basically sound designs, covering a wide range of duties but special mention must be made of the ubiquitous F-class 0-6-0 of which over 1,000 were delivered to, or built in, India between 1874 and 1922. These were really the early 'maids of all work' on the metre gauge. No fewer than one Continental and ten British builders supplied them and they were the first metre-gauge design to be built in India, at the Ajmer works of the Rajputana Malwar Railway in 1895. It is some testimony to their fitness of purpose and stamina that at least two have survived in industrial service to the present day. They were straightforward 0-6-0 outside cylinder tender engines, with inside valves and link motion and outside frames. They originated with 13in x 20in cylinders and 42in wheels, but were uprated by increasing the cylinder bore to 14in and the wheels to 42½in with a corresponding increase in boiler size, lengthened smokebox and increased tender capacity. One interesting detail of these engines was the adoption of Hall's cranks. Being outside-framed engines, the space available for fitting the cranks onto the ends of the axles was limited and in Hall's design the crank boss was extended inward through the axlebox and formed the journal surface. Even with this design there was a tendency for cranks to split or come loose on the axles and, in latter years, many were to be found with shrink-rings round the oval webs to strengthen them.

In the meantime, whilst the metre gauge continued with a basically standard range of engines, the broad gauge tended to proliferate

The Sone Bridge, near Arrah, on the East Indian Railway, completed in 1863. From a watercolour painted *c.* 1865.

its range as duties became increasingly onerous and the whims and ingenuity of individual engineers were brought to bear on new problems. Some of the results were outstandingly successful, others were disastrous, and it is worth noting that the simplest solutions usually provided the best results in the long run.

Before commenting on successes or failures, the conditions prevailing during the first fifty years of Indian railway history should be considered. When the railways started, the indigenous coal was considered, as it indeed was, inferior to the selected grades of steam coal on which the design of locomotive boilers and fireboxes was based in Britain. This led to a continued use of narrow fireboxes of both round-topped and subsequently Belpaire designs, for which vast tonnages of coal were imported from the pits of Britain which produced suitable grades. Ridiculous as this may sound, it must be remembered that there was thus formed a lucrative business in export and shipping, which tended to discourage any serious and immediate attempt to rely on indigenous supplies. It was only on some of the metre- and narrow-gauge lines that the availability of plentiful supplies of timber and the rising cost of imported steam coal led to the adoption of wood-burning, with heightened tender-rails and spark-arresting chimneys as the outward signs.

On the broad gauge, in particular, there was a wide range of duties to be performed. The East Indian Railway enjoyed extensive mileage of substantially level track; the Great Indian Peninsula had to contend with two relatively short, but heavily graded sections up the Bhore and Thull Ghats, the North Western lines had to face continuous heavily graded lines up towards the frontier, with difficult alignment and little need or chance of anything approaching high speeds. Thus, whilst the 2-4-0 and 4-4-0 configurations proved adequate for the passenger duties on the plains, with the 0-6-0 type handling freight, there was need for much more tractive effort on the heavy grades of the G.I.P.R. and the N.W.R. The G.I.P.R. tackled the problem of short-term assistance up (and down) the Ghats by the use of a series of ungainly banking engines carrying their water supplies in huge extended saddle tanks to improve adhesion and equalise axle-loading.

On the Punjab Northern State Railway (later part of the N.W.R.) the problem was solved by the introduction of an outstanding design, the L-class 4-6-0 tender engine, which was introduced in 1880. These engines were built to the specification of Sir Guildford Molesworth, initially by Neilson & Co. of Glasgow, whose influence in detail design is strongly apparent. They were straightforward 4-6-0 engines with inclined outside cylinders and inside valve gear. They were subsequently uprated from their original boiler pressure of 140lb/sq in to 160lb/sq in, with larger wheels (from 50in to 60½in) in which form they became versatile mixed traffic engines on the Nizam's guaranteed State Railway. Altogether, some 355 of these rugged, powerful engines were delivered to India from 1880 to 1913.

Whilst some engineers were solving their problems by the logical extensions of existing practice, others were indulging in less successful flights of fancy. In the face of the high cost of imported coal, thoughts turned to compounding as an aid to economy. In 1883, Sandiford, locomotive superintendent on the Scinde, Punjab & Delhi Railway was experimenting with a four-cylinder 2-4-0 compound and also a two-cylinder conversion of a sister engine. It is interesting to note that these experiments, undertaken in the remoteness of North Western territory, antedated the French development of the balanced four-cylinder compound and were contemporary with T. W. Wordsell's work on the North Eastern Railway in Britain. But the work on the North Western Railway was never taken through to fruition and, in the meantime, a batch of ten Webb three-cylinder uncoupled 2-2-2-0 passenger engines was delivered to the Oudh and Rohilkund Railway, where John Riekie appears on the scene. Riekie was a strong exponent of compounding, but disagreed rather forcefully with other people's approach to the problem. He altered the cylinder proportions and coupled the wheels of one of the Webb compounds and duly claimed to have improved it. Next, having moved to Sukkur, on the North Western Railway, we find him converting engines to two-cylinder compound operation with a complicated system for automatic shortening of the high-pressure cut-off as soon as the engine had started. He finally produced what must have been the most extraordinary fantasy to appear on Indian railways. About the year 1900 he designed an outrageous 2-4-0 with 8ft 0in driving wheels and a three-cylinder triple-expansion front-end. As if this was not enough, steam was supplied by a triple-drum fire tube boiler, with two small drums side-by-side at the bottom and a larger one along the top. Precisely what this device was intended to achieve that the L-class was not already achieving with great competence is hard to imagine. It vanished without trace and one is left with the sad feeling that the long hot nights, devoid of human company and distraction had taken charge of his imagination! He is last heard of early in the 1900s with the North British Locomotive Company taking out patents for valve gears of incredible complexity and dubious reliability.

But whilst Riekie and some of his colleagues were giving rein to their flights of fancy, others were taking a more practical attitude to development. One of the penalties of individualism amongst the various railways was a lack of interchangeability of stock between lines and regions of the country. This problem was particularly acute when strategic needs called for large movements of men and materials across India. Locomotives became a liability when moved out of their home region to others where parts differed in detail and were not interchangeable.

In 1903, a range of standard designs was evolved under the auspices of the British Engineering Standard Association (B.E.S.A.) in collaboration with the consultants, Rendle, Palmer & Tritton. These designs concentrated on standardisation of all main components, with a degree of interchangeability between different types, whilst allowing some degree of latitude in terms of detail to accommodate prevailing conditions on various railways. It was a significant step, taken not without opposition from some of the more entrenched and individualistic opinions. It resulted in a range of sound and workmanlike designs, very British in character, which were to serve the Indian railway system for many years. The designs embraced a range of 4-4-0 and 4-6-0 passenger engines, with 0-6-0 and 2-8-0 freight engines and other variants for specific but numerically less significant duties. In the course of time, these designs were brought up to date by the introduction of superheating, piston valves, outside cylinders and Walschaert's valve gear. Many of these served the railways well beyond the second world war.

Although the basic motive power for the broad- and metre-gauge lines achieved a high degree of standardisation at a relatively early stage in the life of the railways, there was still ample opportunity for the adoption of non-standard designs for specific duties and this led to a fascinating variety, much of which has happily been recorded or preserved for posterity.

In the early years of the present century, several railways adopted the 4-4-2 Atlantic wheel arrangement as power requirements rose to handle the increased weight and speed of the 'mail' trains, and perhaps the finest of these were the elegant and successful four-cylinder de Glehn compounds of the Bengal-Nagpur Railway K-class, a design which was in later years, extended with equal success to the M-class 4-6-2 Pacifics.

But it is to the minor railways, and the hill railways in particular, that one must look for the really individual and unique designs. Pride of place must go to the outstanding B-class 0-4-0 tank engines of the Darjeeling-Himalayan Railway. These little fourteen-ton engines exemplify the basic simple steam locomotive at its best and it is significant that within ten years of the formation of the Company in 1879, a design had evolved which has remained unsurpassed for its duty some ninety years later. Only the quality of the coal available has influenced their performance over the years, their permitted load having been reduced from thirty-two tons to twenty-five tons. The adoption of this simple, straightforward design is surely a classic example of clear thinking, and nothing could be more suited to the line conditions, operating requirements and maintenance facilities.

An equally successful solution, though far more novel and complex in design is to be found on the Matheran Light Railway. Although much shorter than the Darjeeling-Himalayan Railway (12.6 miles compared with 54 miles), its ruling gradient is more severe and its curvature sharper, being in places down to forty-five feet radius. To accommodate this tortuous line, four fully articulated 0-6-0 tank engines were built for the opening of the line in 1907. These are the only known survivors of the type of engine developed by Sir Arthur Haywood at Duffield Bank in Derbyshire in the late 1870s and it is testimony to the soundness of the design and construction that the class is in full operational condition over seventy years later. Here, as on the Darjeeling-Himalayan Railway, the duty has been reduced with the lowering of coal quality, and the engines have lost their original Riggenbach compressive braking system.

The third of the hill railways worthy of special note is the Nilagiri Railway. Whilst the Darjeeling and Matheran Railways operate on the 2ft oin gauge, largely dictated by the terrain and resultant tight curvature, with gradients limited to a maximum of 1:20, the Nilagiri Railway climbs from Mettupalayam to Ootacamund by way of a metre-gauge track some twenty-nine miles long. Of this, thirteen miles operate on the ABT rack principle with a ruling gradient of 1:12.28, the remainder being operated by adhesion with a ruling gradient of 1:23.81. This line was opened in stages, from Mettupalayam on the plain to Coonoor in 1899 and from Coonoor to Ootacamund in 1908. By 1920, the railway had standardised their motive power on the impressive X-class 0-8-2 tank engines which were designed to operate as two-cylinder simple engines on the adhesion sections with a second set of cylinders being brought into operation as the low pressure stage of a four-cylinder compound to drive the rack wheels on the steeply graded sections. These engines, designed and built by the Swiss Locomotive Works, are fascinating in action, having all four cylinders outside, with the low pressure engine above

Fairy Queen. One of a pair of 2-2-2 well-tank engines built by Kitson, Thompson and Hewitson in 1855 for the East Indian Railway. This engine finished work in 1908 and is now preserved in full working order in the Rail Transport Museum, Delhi.

the high pressure and driving two separate coupled crankshafts above and between the second and third axles. These crankshafts rotate backwards in relation to the driving wheels when on the rack section and this, coupled with the two sets of Walschaert's valve gear, produces a truly spectacular display in action. This railway is unique in one other respect of its operation. The engines propel the trains up the gradient and lead them down in order to minimise the risk of breakaway in the event of a parted coupling. This practice, together with the provision of manual and vacuum braking on the rolling stock for both the rack and adhesion axles and of steam and Riggenbach compressive braking on the engines, leaves little to chance in terms of operating safety.

Not all the railways built in India conformed to the traditional theme and some weird and wonderful minor transport systems were conceived around the turn of the century. The great advantage of a railway over other forms of land transport is the ease with which a smooth metal wheel will roll on a smooth metal rail. In other words, a relatively small effort can move relatively large loads compared with the effort required with other combinations of wheel and road. The traditional interpretation of the railway is a pair of accurately spaced steel rails on which roll wheels with flanges on the inside to maintain the necessary guidance. This scheme relies on the accurate relationship of the rails by the use of sleepers which maintain the gauge and distribute the load on the ground. This type of track is relatively expensive to lay and requires continuous attention to maintain its condition.

For applications where lines are only required to handle light loads, where speed is not an important factor and where frequent changes of route may be required (as on construction sites or plantations), other solutions to the problem were developed which yielded most of the advantages of the metal wheel-on-rail combination with considerable reductions in first cost and subsequent maintenance. These solutions were based on the monorail principle, whereby only one rail was laid, with various alternative means for balancing the load upon it. The obvious advantages were that a given quantity of rail would stretch twice as far and there would be no problems involved with the maintenance of the gauge between rails. Guidance was provided by providing a flange on each side of the wheel to straddle the head of the rail.

Pioneer of such systems in India seems to have been a man by the name of Addis, an English engineer practising in India. Addis took

out patents for his Cart and Wheel in 1868 although there is no evidence that this first invention of his actually ran on a rail. Nevertheless, as a predecessor to his next invention, the description, from the Professional Papers on Indian Engineering (Roorkee) 1873, is worth quoting:

Certainly one of the most useful models in this room [at the Akola Exhibition] was 'Addis' patent 'Cart and Wheel'. It comprises two essential points, first the wheels are formed of segmentary parts of wrought iron, circumferenced by felloes and tied in the usual manner; the nave is flush with the spokes, thus lessening the risk of collision. Among the advantages possessed by this invention, the wheel is calculated to be durable, and easier of construction. The two axels [sic], six inches in length, work in journals and are easily arranged in case of damage. Another palpable advantage is that the pole is so arranged as to admit of the cart being drawn back without the necessity of turning while it can be wholly withdrawn, passed through the centre of the box in the body of the cart, which contains a tent, and used as a tent pole, while the platform can be used for sleeping on a swampy locality.

Mr Addis apparently made several varieties of carts for military, sporting and other uses, some being fitted with bell-shaped tents; as also road watering carts, night-soil carts; the prices at Tanna (Thana) near Bombay ranging from Rs150 to Rs350.

Doubtless, Mr Addis found the effort to move his carts to be a drawback, for he then turned his inventive talents to placing them on rail. In 1872 the (London) *Public Opinion* carried a notice of this principle:

The importance of an extremely cheap system of railway capable of providing outlying districts with better means of reaching the existing lines and of facilitating transit in towns, has long been recognised by Engineers, and it appears that such a system has now been devised . . . The invention . . . of Mr Addis. The locomotive weighs four tons, and has two wheels running bicycle fashion on the rail; two other wheels in the usual position, and with caoutchouc [unvulcanised rubber] tyres. The engineer can throw the weight on the rail wheels or the road wheels, at pleasure, the latter increasing the bite and facilitating the ascent of an incline; there is 1 in 33 on the trial line. The rail weighs about 15lb to the yard and does not rise above the roadway. A speed of 8–11 miles per hour is attained, the motion is smooth and pleasant and no difficulty is experienced in turning very sharp curves.

Addis claimed that forty men could lay a mile of track in one day and that the cost per mile would be Rs6,220 (£650). The carrying capacity was claimed to be six times as much, per pair of bullocks, as an ordinary cart on the road! Unfortunately, no record exists of any practical applications of the principle though doubtless it was adopted and used until ousted by more conventional systems.

The next, and only successful interpretation of the monorail principle in India was the Ewing system. Ewing was another English engineer who turned his mind to solving the low cost railway problem. He adopted the compromise solution of laying a single rail and fitting not less than two double-flanged wheels, line-ahead under the vehicle. To stabilise it, he fitted an outrigger, about 5 feet long on one side with an iron wheel about three feet diameter and six inches wide on the end and resting on the ground. Some 95 per cent of the weight was to be on the rail and 5 per cent on the outrigger, thus obtaining most of the advantages of low resistance. Ewing took out various patents in the 1890s and there are at least three recorded uses of his system. In 1902, a monorail on his system was installed in the High Range in South India for handling tea and other freight to the Top Station whence an aerial ropeway provided a link with Keranganie, some 6,400 feet below on the plain. This monorail was operated by ponies until it was superseded, in 1908, by a conventional light railway.

About the same period, probably in 1900, Colonel C. W. Bowles, engineer in charge of the building of the Kharagpur Workshops of the Bengal-Nagpur Railway, adopted the Ewing system in substitution for the conventional contractors' light railway for handling materials on the site. His experience must have been satisfactory for in 1907, by which time he had become the Engineer to the State of Patiala in the Punjab, he started to build permanent lines as part of the State transport system. Two quite separate stretches of line were installed. One was fifteen miles long, from Sirhind on the North Western Railway, to Morinda; the other from Patiala City out towards Sunam, some thirty miles to the west. The former section was operated, in spite of difficulties of one sort or another, from 1907 until 1927 and throughout this period, the motive power was provided either by mules of the State Army, or by bullocks.

The latter section, from Patiala seems only to have operated until 1914 and it is doubtful whether the projected terminus at Sunam was ever reached. This section was, however, operated jointly by animal power and four extraordinary steam locomotives. By the greatest of good fortune, the locomotives and rolling stock were not destroyed following the closure of this line, and some sixty years later it has been possible to rescue and restore one locomotive and one coach (Colonel Bowles' private saloon) which are now on display, in operational condition, in the Rail Transport Museum in Delhi.

Colonel Bowles must have been an enterprising engineer because in the 1920s he was experimenting with a petrol-driven locomotive on the Sirhind section. To him may well be accorded the credit of introducing the first locally built internal-combustion locomotive on the Indian sub-continent! So ended the history of the Ewing system

The short-lived Ewing monorail in the High Range displays its first-class passenger accommodation. The coach runs on two double flanged wheels set in line and the outrigger and stabiliser wheel run on the ground on the far side.

in India, but happily not without trace. Whilst the development of road transport was undoubtedly the prime cause of its decline, the grooves worn in the ground by the continuous passage of the outrigger over the same path led to ~~some~~ bizarre situations, and aggravated the problem of maintenance. But the character of the undertaking is immortalised in its title The Patiala State Monorail Trainway.

1927 would have seen the end of the monorail story but for one final fling which lasted six years and finally sank, literally, without trace. Strictly, it falls outside the period of this book, but should be included to complete the story.

In 1946, Mr A. W. C. Skelton, then Chief Engineer to the Jamnagar-Dwarka Railway in Saurashtra, designed and built an eleven mile stretch on the Skelton guideway principle from Khambalia to Bhanvad. His system consisted of a concrete roadway on which ran a diesel-driven locomotive on four rubber-tyred wheels. Along the centre of the roadway ran a single rail which steered the locomotive and carried the bulk of the weight of the trailing vehicles which were fitted with stabiliser wheels on either side. Transmission troubles dogged the locomotive and the tyres were unequal to the duty. In 1952, a dam was constructed across the Ghee River, the waters rose and the last monorail went to a watery grave.

A certain Mr Landon, passing through Hyderabad about seventy years ago, lamented that 'of all the dreary stations in this land Wadi is the dreariest'. It was typical of so many small stations in the remote areas of India: a roof of corrugated iron spanning a few rooms that served as an office and a waiting room, but because Wadi was a junction on the line between Madras and Bombay it also boasted a refreshment room. Most wayside stations were little more than shanties with some adjacent huts for the native railway staff and a slightly grander one for the stationmaster. The waiting rooms, when they were provided on such stations, were less for the comfort of passengers and more for the convenience of engineers and other railway officials who used them for overnight accommodation while on duty. Some could be very spartan.

The waiting room was like nothing I had seen before [recalled Olive Douglas in 1913]. A large, dirty, barn-like apartment with some cane seats arranged round the wall, and an attempt at a dressing-table, with a spotty looking-glass on it, in one corner. One small lamp, smelling vilely, served to make darkness visible, and an old hag crouching at the door was the attendant spirit.

Officials spent much time on inspection tours and were occasionally accompanied by their wives in inspection saloons. Where short forays were involved, a push-trolley was employed. Mrs Helen Westropp, whose husband was in the Indian Civil Service, experiences this form of transport near Bombay around the year 1900.

Larger stations were better equipped with separate rooms for men and women and adjoining washrooms and bathrooms. The floors were usually clean enough for bedding to be placed on them.

In 1854 the Madras Government approved a proposal by the railway company to classify stations into four groups. Stations used extensively by Europeans were to be designated first and second class; large towns would qualify for third-class stations and small stations with few passengers would be relegated to the fourth and lowest class. Waiting rooms for fourth-class stations were considered unnecessary.

Shelter from the weather is all we require [said the Consulting Engineer for Railways], and an open shed with one office attached, and a wall with door, and a barred window or two separating it from the platform would be the best arrangement.

These primitive conditions were to be only marginally better in third-class stations where the booking office would be enlarged to serve the additional function as a refuge for the few Europeans who might be passing through.

The discomfort endured by the majority of users of the railways, that is the Indian population, prompted the Governor-General to issue a Circular in 1864 urging an improvement in the comfort and convenience of all passengers. Basic facilities like lavatories should be installed in every station; the more important stations should also have refreshment rooms and seraies (accommodation for travellers). The Deputy Consulting Engineer of the N.E. Extension of the Great Indian Peninsula Railway considered waiting rooms, or at least sheds, for third-class passengers to be a more urgent priority than refreshment rooms. The report of the East Indian Railway for 1865 deplored the inadequate number of third-class ticket offices, even in large stations like Jamalpur and Cawnpore, resulting in uncontrollable crowds fighting and struggling to purchase their tickets from a solitary clerk.

The siting of railway stations was to a large extent decided by the distribution of the population, the centres of industry and the nature of the terrain. The Madras Railway in 1854 contemplated building stations of varying size every five or six miles. After the Mutiny of 1857, however, a new factor taken into consideration was their strategic and defensible position.

In 1864 the Government of India drew the attention of local governors to the importance of placing stations where they could get the immediate support of troops in time of trouble and of arranging the

Army manoeuvres at Panipat in 1884. Walsh Lovatt and Co. were agents in India for light railway systems designed for portability and are here demonstrating one to the Army for their supply lines. The locomotive is Bagnall no. 511, *Sirdar*, and cost £408/5/-.

complex of station buildings as compactly as possible to make their defence easier.

In general, an enclosure of some kind is demanded for purposes of ordinary security, and an enclosure wall (with iron gates to close openings) affording no footing on its summit, and flanked by towers or other buildings adapted to give a musketry fire, of which, considering the range of the rifle, there need be very few, and with the exterior cleared of cover for some space around, is all that is really required or contemplated by the Government of India.

Lahore Station was designed like a fortress by William Brunton, the Chief Engineer of the Amritsar and Multan Railway. When the site of this station was debated in 1854 it was at first agreed to locate it within the cantonment near the barracks. But the case put forward by Brunton for 'a passenger station, which shall be perfectly defensive in every respect' prevailed. Opened in 1864 with long massive walls, pierced with loop-holes for muskets, flanked by bomb-proof towers and crowned by turrets, with heavy sliding doors which could close the rail exits, it looked more like a medieval castle than a station.

The railways engineers who designed many of the stations usually constructed them in the simplest form without any decorative embellishments. When a professional architect was commissioned in 1866 to design a new station in Madras, the Board of the Railway Company stipulated that 'beyond the beauty of a good design, which may not cost more in execution than a bad one, all ornamentation should be avoided, and the building be as simple as consists with its purpose and situation.' One would like to think that they had been persuaded by John Ruskin's admonition in his *Seven Lamps of Architecture* (1849):

Better bury gold in the embankments than put it in ornaments on the stations ... Railroad architecture has, or would have, a dignity of its own, if it were only left to its work.

The *Calcutta Review* for 1861 wondered why

stations [were] built in the North West Provinces, that would make fit palaces for the Governor-General, and who are they for? For the 1,500,000 passengers whose pride is to be half naked, but are favored with these luxuries, we presume, to induce them to improve a little upon their domestic architecture.

Most railway stations in India today comprise office accommodation and waiting rooms flanked by platforms that may or may not be covered. They are utilitarian in design and modest in size. There are, of course, exceptions, the most distinguished being the celebrated Victoria Terminus in Bombay. Built as the terminus and headquarters of the Great Indian Peninsula Railway and opened on the

Lahore Railway Station in 1864.

Details of the Gothic architecture of the Victoria Terminus and administrative building, Bombay.

occasion of Queen Victoria's Golden Jubilee, some of its monumentality and magnificence is hidden by the buildings that now hem it in. The architect, F. W. Stevens, conceived it as a blend of Venetian Gothic and Indo-Islamic styles. Its proportions rival those of a cathedral with a huge central dome complemented by a number of smaller ones. Carved stone, glazed tiles, brasswork and wrought iron, stained glass windows, polished Aberdeen granite columns and groups of sculptured figures huddled above each principal gable coalesce in an exuberance of ornament and vitality. 'Much too magnificent for a bustling crowd of railway passengers', was the prim judgment of the former Vicereine, Lady Dufferin, in 1889.

Although the Victoria Terminus dwarfs all other stations, there are a number that are still impressive. Howrah Station, built in the 1850s as the East Indian Railway terminus for Calcutta, was rebuilt in 1906 with an imposing red brick façade and is probably the largest station in the land. Economy dictated its location on the west bank of the Hooghly river linked, as we have seen, by ferry and pontoon bridge with Calcutta.

There was one large station in Calcutta, the Sealdah terminus of the Eastern Bengal Railway (1862), which stood apart from the general style of station architecture prevailing in India. This was the work of the famous English engineer, Isambard Kingdom Brunel, and it exhibited an Italianate profile tinged with the Orient and had the characteristic low-pointed roof of which many fine examples were to be found on the Great Western Railway in England. The original Brunel station at Sealdah no longer exists.

Throughout the line of the East Indian Railway, from Lucknow to Delhi, even relatively minor stations exhibit considerable architectural treatment, with a skilful blending of Indo-Islamic domes and arches and a sensible functionalism. In general, regional styles of architecture were adopted for all but the least significant structures throughout the land, although in the northern areas which had been particularly influenced by the mutiny and aggression on the frontier, the style was markedly influenced by the need for fortification and defence. Thus, many of the bridges, tunnels and stations exhibit characteristics reminiscent of a medieval castle rather than a railway station.

Once the railways had passed the experimental stage, it was necessary to plan for a railway system as a whole, for which one of the essentials is workshop capacity to undertake the building and repairs of locomotives, rolling stock, signalling equipment and other hard-

Victoria Terminus at the end of the nineteenth century.

ware. Just as the great railway towns of Crewe and Swindon grew up round the newly established works of railways in Britain, so new townships, with a pattern and character of their own, sprang up, sometimes in remote places, to provide the Indian counterpart.

In some cases the workshops were built in or around the headquarters towns of the railways, but in others, remote sites were selected where completely new townships had to be built with all the services and facilities to support the workshop and its workforce. Typical of the latter policy was the railway township of Jamalpur, main workshop of the East Indian Railway. Jamalpur lies on the northern edge of the state of Bihar, on the south bank of the Ganges and about 250 miles north-west of Calcutta. The area was selected for the building of this major works for two reasons. Firstly, the area was well known for the skill and industry of its local craftsmen who traditionally had worked metal, particularly silver, in the manufacture of utensils and ornaments. Secondly, the view was held that a workshop divorced from the distractions and competition of a town such as Calcutta would achieve better results. The workforce would be much more dependent on the Company and training to new standards of engineering would not be wasted by loss of skilled men to a growing competitive market.

Here then, at Jamalpur the main workshops were built for the East Indian Railway in 1862. Wholly unfettered by existing boundary limitations or high cost land, their layout was on a very expansive scale. Buildings were designed to undertake every aspect of overhaul and repair of the railway's stock of locomotives. Steam provided the motive power for all the machinery and the range of capabilities was comprehensive. Although not designed to manufacture new locomotives, Jamalpur had started building in the 1880s, making all the parts with the exception of wheels, which were still imported. Some reservation must be placed on the early claims for building new locomotives, since liberal quotas of spares were shipped out to India for maintenance and replacement purposes. If these were not consumed as rapidly as had been budgeted, stocks accumulated and were, perhaps somewhat unofficially, assembled into additional complete units.

The boards of the railway companies and the consultants, with their long-range view of the situation from London, did not always advocate or provide the type of locomotive which the operating staff required to do the job in India and the surplus of spare parts provided a means of overcoming the handicap. At the turn of the century, Mogulpura workshops, at Lahore, needed a shunting tank engine which was not immediately forthcoming from their masters in England. They designed and produced the first six examples by taking parts for a 0-6-0 design, adding a set of tender wheels, making side-tanks and bunker, and thus creating a neat 0-6-2T, classified ST. The first six, built at Mogulpura in 1904 justified their existence and a further 41 were subsequently produced for them by the North British Locomotive Company. But, with the notable exception of Ajmer, Indian workshops did not build their own locomotives in the accepted sense.

By the 1880s, Jamalpur had grown into a major workshop employing upwards of 5,000 men and by 1906 the total approached 10,000. They and their families were based in the appropriate grade and standard of housing forming part of the township which the Company laid out, with geometric precision, around the works. With typical Victorian loyalty streets were named according to the custom of the age: Church Street, King's Road, Queen's Road, Prince's Road, Victoria Road, Albert Road, with Steam Road through the length of the town to bring one back to reality. Apprentices, European or Eurasian, were well catered for in an extensive training school and residential quarters. Churches of every denomination existed for the various religious preferences of the several hundred Christians who commanded the more senior positions.

Social life centred round the clubs and institutes. The railways maintained a volunteer defence force (the Railway Volunteers) and it was a virtual condition of service that staff should volunteer to serve. They provided such sabre-rattling as might be necessary, but, apart from twice-weekly drill parades, their chief function was probably the dispensing of appropriate light music by their band in the evenings and at week-ends.

Kipling recorded the scene in 1888:

The Company does everything and owns everything. The gallant apprentice may be a wild youth with an earnest desire to go occasionally 'on the bend'. But three times a week between 7 & 8 p.m. he must attend the night school and sit at the feet of M. Bonnand who teaches him mechanics and statistics so thoroughly that even the awful Government Inspector is pleased. Best and prettiest of the many good and pretty things in Jamalpur is the Institute on a Saturday when the Volunteer band is playing and the tennis courts are full and the babydom of Jamalpur – fat, sturdy children – frolic round the bandstand. The people dance . . . they act, they play billiards, they study their newspaper, they play cards and everything else. They flirt in a sumptuous building and in the hot weather, the gallant apprentice ducks his friend in the swimming bath. Decidedly, the railway folk make their lives pleasant.

In the middle of the maidan, under the shade of a banyan tree, is a solitary grave. The inscription on the headstone read (for it was stolen in 1977):

Thomas Oulam Roberts, formerly of Vulcan Foundry. Foreman Jamalpur Erecting Works. Died 1864 after an untimely encounter with a tiger. Aged 27 years.

Nearby is a mound, said to be the grave of the tiger.

Pleasures and pains of travel

A journey on the railways of India has never been merely a convenient means of getting to one's destination; it is also a vivid experience, rich and life-enhancing or traumatic and nerve-racking, depending upon one's point of view and equanimity. The confident verdict of one satisfied passenger after travelling from Howrah to Chinsurah on the East Indian Railway in 1854 was that 'this new mode of travelling will soon supersede every other in India'. With remarkable speed the railway lines spread out tentacles from the Presidency cities of Bombay, Calcutta and Madras, gradually linking all the main towns. Few people spared any regrets for the passing of the horse-drawn gharry which for years had bumped and swayed its passengers over uneven and potholed roads, transforming any lengthy journey into an exercise of grim endurance. By 1861–2 the number of passengers who had been carried over the 700 miles of track already laid was 61,817 (first class), 299,820 (second class) and 6,477,055 (third class), the last figure representing Indians who, after an initial hesitation, accepted the railways as the natural way to travel. One cynical comment made at the time was that Indians readily took to the railways when they realised that 'instead of travelling for five weary days on the road, they would get to their journey's end in about seven hours and, all the while – delightful state to the Hindoo – do nothing but sit'.

Europeans travelled first and second class in a degree of comfort that compared quite favourably with that available on trains in England. Louis Rousselet who arrived in India in 1864 and made good use of the railways during his six years' stay recollected that

thanks to the sleeping carriages, I had been able to travel over this immense distance with comparatively little fatigue – sleeping at night on a comfortable little bed, and walking up and down in my carriage during the day; and, at stations, unprovided with buffets, I found a servant who, when he had taken the orders for my meal, telegraphed on to the next station, where my breakfast or dinner awaited my arrival.

In the 1860s first-class fares on the East Indian Railway were double those of second class but second-class carriages with their cane seats and wooden backs were more comfortable in hot weather than the cushioned and leather seats of the first class. On the standard 5ft 6in gauge railways, first-class compartments by the end of the century had become quite spacious (the floor area being about 12ft by 8ft) with accommodation for six seated passengers or four sleeping. The seats, about 6ft long and 2ft wide, were placed on either side of the compartment and could be easily converted into sleeping berths. Above were two more berths which were fastened up during the day, and let down at night. Attached to each compartment was a lavatory which on some lines also had room for a small bath. Opening from the compartment was a smaller room for a servant whose services according to Murray's *Handbook* were indispensable. He served meals and drinks, made the beds and looked after the mountain of luggage that inevitably accompanied the first-class passenger: portmanteaux, suitcases, dressing-bag, hat-box, helmet-case, lunch-basket and a huge roll of bedding. All the guide-books cautioned the traveller always to have his own bedding made up of a razai or wadded quilt, two pairs of blankets thick and thin, pillows and perhaps an eiderdown, all contained in a canvas or waterproof cover.

The Railway Companies, ever attentive to the comfort of their first-class passengers, tried various ways of cooling the coaches before air-conditioning was introduced in 1936. Louis Rousselet travelled from Bombay to Calcutta in a compartment with matting made of sweet-smelling grass known as khas khas tatties hanging down the windows which were 'kept moist by reservoirs specially provided for the purpose. This moisture, enveloping the carriage', Rousselet confirmed, 'preserves the temperature at a degree of coolness sufficient almost to extinguish the risk of incurring sun-stroke or apoplexy, at one time so frequent on these journeys.'

One device developed by R. D. Saunders for the Great Indian Peninsula Railway in 1872 incorporated a large rectangular duct running from end to end of the coach under the floor. At each end, the duct enlarged into a funnel, the leading one being open to scoop up the air, and the trailing one closed. In the duct were layers of khas khas matting kept damp by intermittent douches of water from a tank on the carriage roof, regulated by a tipple-bucket device fitted to the carriage ends. The hot air (and dust) entering the duct was filtered and cooled by evaporation as it passed through the khas khas and was led through openings in the floor of the carriage. When an electric fan was fitted in carriages, it was soon discovered that its effectiveness was markedly improved by placing a large tub of ice beneath it. Of course, an ever-present palliative was ice and soda brought by an attentive servant at frequent intervals.

By the beginning of the twentieth century most of the long-distance trains had restaurant cars, but for shorter journeys and on local lines it was customary to dine at refreshment rooms at certain stations where trains halted three times a day for about half an hour. Meals, which could be ordered in advance by the guard, were usually ready to be served with impressive speed and efficiency as soon as the train arrived. On those lines where such refreshment rooms were far apart a luncheon-basket was deemed indispensable. E. Reynolds-Ball in *The Tourist's India* (1907) was certain that nothing less than 'cold chicken, biscuits, potted meats, Swiss milk, Brand's Essence and tea' would assuage the hungry traveller. Discounting the heat and the dust (the carriages were never particularly clean) first-class travel provided a standard of luxurious living that few European railways could match.

Soda water is offered to you just as you are conceiving the wish for it [Oscar Browning in *Impressions of Indian Travel* (1903) wistfully recalled]. Tea comes to you punctually at 6 am and as often as you may desire it during the rest of the day. No sooner have you passed your hand over your stubbly beard than a barber appears to shave you in the carriage. You get a 'little breakfast' of eggs and bacon, with bananas and oranges at eight, a delightful tiffin in the heat of noon, and a good dinner at sunset.

As night came on and the oil lamps were lit (gas lamps were introduced during the 1870s), the passenger having dined reasonably well could settle to enjoy the latest batch of stories by Kipling in Wheeler's Railway Library series. In 1902 the Jodhpur Railway became the first company in India to instal electric lights in the carriages.

There used to be a saying in Rajputana that nothing was slower than a Jodhpur train, but most Europeans agreed that all the trains were far too slow. 'The white man is often in a hurry, the native never: the Indian train strolls accordingly at a decorous twenty miles an hour', observed one exasperated visitor to India. 'A train

Sikh woodcut of a railway train *c.* 1870. The engine is evidently a wood-burner.

can scarcely travel 300 miles on the East Indian Railway without being from two to three hours late', grumbled the *Calcutta Review* in 1867. Prolonged stops at stations were normally blamed for these delays. 'Every train (except mails) stops at every station a quarter of an hour for purposes of gossip, and at all large stations half an hour or an hour' was the trying experience of R. Palmer (*A Little Tour in India* 1913) who was completely disenchanted with the Indian railway system. 'A vile business' was his emphatic opinion. Completely unmoved by the sights, sounds and smells of the colourful life that congregated in and around the railway stations and packed the third- and fourth-class carriages, he dismissed all non-Europeans as 'a very dirty and malodorous horde of men and women'.

The introduction and development of railways in India was opposed by those people in England as well as in India who believed that Indians would never be induced to travel on them because of the contamination of castes. Although this did not happen third-class carriages did nothing to remove caste barriers. In 1874 one Hindu deplored the fact that the railways seated 'the sweepers, the *chamars*, and the like classes of people in the same carriage along with the Hindustanis of the higher order'. A Muslim paper in Lucknow pressed for the provision of 'separate carriages for the respectable classes of the Hindus and Musselmans on the one hand and the lower classes of the natives on the other'. But all the railway companies were impervious to such entreaties. As early as 1854 the Chief Engineer of the Madras Railway said it was not the responsibility of the railways to recognise 'the distinctions of creed and caste, so as to provide one carriage for a Brahmin, and another for a Pariah'. The only distinction he recommended was that 'which can be purchased by money'.

When the first trains thundered through the Indian countryside, simple natives were in awe of the 'fire-carriages' and according to the *Overland Telegraph and Courier* (16 April 1853) 'they salaamed the omnipotence of steam as it passed.' Villagers reasoned that an engine which could move in either direction without any visible help must surely be a god. So in great deference they put the sacred red marks or tilaks on the smoke stacks of the engines, left offerings of food and money on the footplate and placed flowers on the track. Even educated Indians felt some initial apprehension about their safety on trains. According to the *Bengal Hurkaru* (23 August 1854) a Bengal scholar having resolved to make a trip on the Calcutta line,

duly consulted the stars with the help of the Almanac, and fixed upon Thursday for the journey as a 'lucky' day. He fortified himself for the expedition by bathing three times in

RAILWAY TRAVELLING IN INDIA.

First-class compartment for Europeans on the Indian Railways. Note the dog under the
bed. (L. Rousselet *India and its Native Princes*, London 1882.)

the river, and repeating the name of his tutelar god 937 times . . . He went as far as Hooghly but declined to undertake the return journey, because, said he, too much travelling in the car of fire is calculated to shorten life, for seeing that it annihilates time and space and curtails the length of every other journey, shall it not also shorten the journey of human life?

Another nervous traveller

felt a sort of vertigo and a dizziness come over him. He looked down on the ground out of the window of the carriage when the giddiness increased the more, and went on increasing at every station, although he stopped to refresh himself wherever he could procure the means of doing so – till at length by the time [he] returned to Howrah, his speech was 'thick' and he could hardly keep his legs, so that his friends were obliged to bring him across in a palky [a closed four-wheel horse carriage].

But once this fear and suspicion of the railways had been dispelled, Indians soon discovered that travel on them was not so much a disagreeable necessity as an exhilarating experience. Not even the primitive accommodation of fourth-class carriages with no seating, which were brought into service in 1874, had any effect on the numbers using them. Public agitation secured the installation of benches in

1885 when the original third class became the intermediate class and the fourth was renamed the third class.

The original third-class carriages normally carried 70 passengers. In 1862 their capacity was increased to 120 on the East Indian and Great Indian Peninsula Railways by the introduction of two-storied carriages: 50 passengers in the lower tier and 70 in the upper. The Report of the East Indian Railway for 1865 expressed cautious satisfaction with these experimental carriages, arguing that 'a native does not want cubic, but superficial space whereon to dispose his bundle, his brass pots, and other property'.

The intolerable overcrowding of third-class carriages was the subject of a stern rebuke in the *Calcutta Review* for 1867.

Huddled and crowded like cattle into carriages often unprovided with seats, the doors are shut and locked upon them, and there they must remain till they arrive at their journey's end. . . . We saw it suggested somewhere the other day that the capacity of the third class carriages on the Punjab Railway had been calculated according to the *weight* of the passengers rather than their accommodation.

An Inspection Report of the East Indian Railway for July 1865 indi-

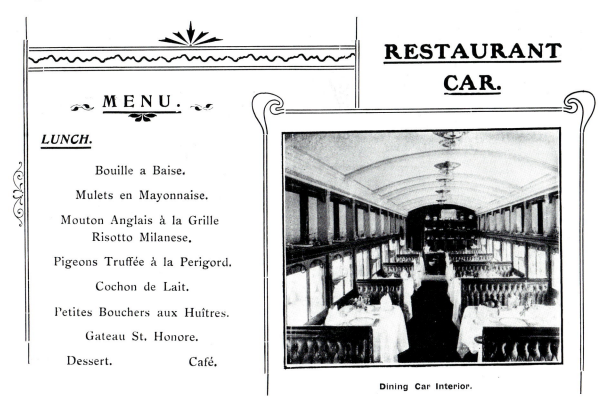

MENU.

LUNCH.

Bouille a Baise.

Mulets en Mayonnaise.

Mouton Anglais à la Grille
Risotto Milanese.

Pigeons Truffée à la Perigord.

Cochon de Lait.

Petites Bouchers aux Huîtres.

Gateau St. Honore.

Dessert.   Café.

RESTAURANT CAR.

Dining Car Interior.

The Great Indian Peninsula Railway took the lead in introducing first-class restaurant cars on its mail trains. The standard was equal to that of British railways of the period. The menu for the inauguration of the service on 23 July 1904 made no concession to the oriental environment.

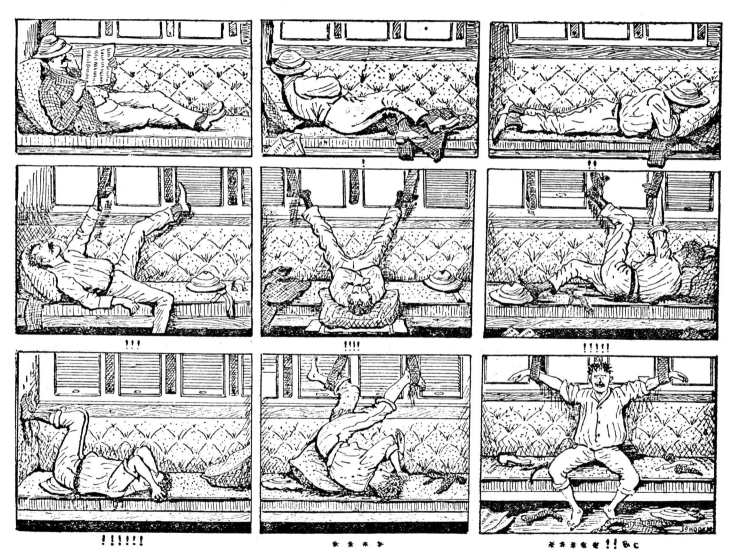

Travel on Indian railways. Trying a variety of postures to break the monotony of a three days' journey.

cates that the authorities were trying to reduce overcrowding by dividing third-class carriages into compartments with a maximum capacity of twelve people. But the Report concluded resignedly that 'natives do travel in parties and that they prefer being crowded to being separated'.

The Government of India was not indifferent to the discomforts endured by Indians who after all formed the bulk of railway passengers. In April 1864 it issued a circular drawing attention to overcrowding in carriages, the lack of adequate lavatory facilities in stations, the need for a supply of food for Indians wherever there were first-class refreshment rooms and the provision of seraies or hostels wherever necessary. It recommended that third- and fourth-class carriages should prominently display their seating capacity and that it should be a regulation of all railway companies that the authorised seating arrangements should be enforced. The Inspection Report of the East Indian Railway for the second quarter of 1866 revealed an improvement in the treatment of third-class passengers: carriage doors were now unlocked at stations 'to enable passengers to descend for the purpose of nature' and food was available at most stations. There was still a need for more waiting rooms and for drinking water to be supplied by persons of acceptable castes.

Over 3,000 signatures were appended to a petition presented to the Viceroy in 1866 by the British Indian Association, North Western Provinces, expressing concern about conditions which imposed 'a dire evil and slavery' upon all third-class passengers. It contrasted the comparatively few rich travellers who enjoyed the comfort of waiting rooms with the thousands who had no shelter while they waited patiently for their trains.

It cannot be expected from them that they should come in only at the proper time. Most of them have an indefinite idea of time, knowing little beyond pruhurs [period of prayer] of three hours each. A large number, too, come in from surrounding villages and rural districts where no time is kept. Besides, the Time-Table of the Railway Company constitutes a study by itself.

Furthermore trains were frequently very late. At this point the petition became eloquent about the misery of these unfortunate travellers.

There is no shelter from the heavy and drenching showers of rain lasting for hours. There is no shelter from the hot winds and clouds of dust. There is no shelter from the cold cutting blast. . . . Many a poor Native's illness or death is traceable to sufferings at a Railway Station while waiting for the train.

Waiting rooms or 'sheds' were recommended along with restaurants suitably divided for Hindus and Muslims, and drinking water rooms

In 1888, A. H. Wheeler and Company launched their Indian Railway Library for travellers to read on long train journeys. Their books included some of the early stories of Rudyard Kipling, such as *Soldiers Three*, *Under the Deodars*, *Wee Willie Winkie*, etc. mainly reprinted from *The Week's News*.

staffed by Brahmins for 'Hindoos of the better castes'. The petition welcomed the chuttrums or seraies which were being constructed by the Madras Railway.

Disquiet, however, was shown about the ill-treatment and loss of honour (hoormut) which Hindus and Muslims alike received from some European fellow-passengers in second-class carriages. These were collectively castigated as 'a low class of Europeans who are servants either "on the tramp" or are permitted by the Railway Company, as being their servants, to travel *free* second class'. A separate carriage was recommended for such undesirable travelling companions. But the petition was not so enthusiastic about separate carriages for women. This segregation apparently sometimes resulted in unfortunate incidents. We are informed 'that a man got in disguise into a carriage set apart for females on the Punjab line, and remained unapprehended during the entire journey', but with what consequences the petition does not reveal. In a passionate peroration the petition deplores the 'peculiar management [of the Railway], the miseries and inconveniences suffered from which, equal often the horrors of the "middle passage".'

Nearly forty years after the presentation of that petition third-class passengers were still complaining about travelling conditions. Overcrowding was still prevalent according to a letter in the South Indian newspaper, *Vrittanta Chintamini* (June 1901) but the lack of adequate toilet facilities was also mentioned. The letter-writer said that third-class passengers had to wait in great discomfort until the train stopped at a station. A certain Mr Sen wrote an indignant letter to the Divisional Office of the East Indian Railway after his embarrassing experience.

I am arrive by passenger train at Ahmedpore station and my belly is too much swelling with jack fruit. I am therefore went to privy. Just as I doing the nuisance, that guard making whistle blow for train to go off and I am running with lotah [brass pot] in one hand and dhotie in the next when I am fall over and expose all my shockings [?] to man and female on platform. I am get leaved at Ahmedpore station. This too much bad, if passenger go to make dung, that dam guard no wait train five minutes for him. I am therefore pray your honour to make big fine on that guard for public sake. Otherwise I am making big report to papers.

Lavatories were not installed in third-class carriages until 1891 but it would appear from a report of the Oudh and Rohilkund Railway in 1902 that even here class distinctions were meticulously observed.

Two-tier third-class carriage of the Bombay, Baroda and Central India Railway. Although on the broad gauge, headroom was at a premium and it was a case of 'sitting' room only. Introduced in 1862, these coaches provided some relief for overcrowding, with a capacity of 120; 50 on the lower deck and 70 on top. (*Illustrated London News*, 12 March 1864.)

An intelligent native passenger, with whom I discussed the design in a 3rd class carriage at Lucknow, pointed to some obvious defects; the arrangement for lighting was poor; the hole in the floor – only 5 inches in diameter – decidedly too small; apparently the designer had taken a first class closet as his standard and had made the diameter of the orifice in proportion to the fare.

Railway stations have always been an irresistible magnet for lower class Indians. There they congregate at all times of the day, queueing to buy tickets, haggling about the price of the ticket, buying chupatties, sticky sweetmeats, hot tea and water from the station vendors, performing their ablutions, and sleeping in the waiting rooms and on the platforms. They arrive hours, perhaps days, before their trains are due but they wait patiently and philosophically. In the early days of the railways they were known to encamp deliberately for several days at the station thinking by this stratagem the weary booking clerk would capitulate and give them cheaper fares. On the other hand, booking clerks were known to charge higher fares and to pocket the difference.

The long stops at stations that so annoyed European passengers were probably unavoidable with so many people on the move, carrying their pots and pans, bedclothes, boxes, trestle-beds and small children. The relatives and friends who came to see them off swelled the crowds. In 1904 nearly 200,000,000 third-class passengers were carried on the railways. Presumably these were the people who bought tickets; the fare-dodgers would have added considerably to that total. Evasion of fares was a relatively petty offence compared with the widespread thieving suffered by the railways right from the start. Professional gangs robbed and occasionally murdered passengers and the introduction of corridor carriages made their criminal activities easier. The Koravars, a low-caste tribe, made a speciality of bag-stealing, substituting their own bags filled with rags. Other thieves were accomplished in the manipulation of long secateurs to remove bracelets and necklaces from sleeping passengers. Villagers, probably compelled by poverty and hunger, helped gangs to plunder large quantities of grain and other foodstuffs from passing trains. An Indian police official in his *Reminiscences* (1898) reluctantly admired their skill in boarding and jumping off moving trains.

Many Indian princes were eager to establish their own railway system or to let railway companies extend their lines through their territory. When the Government of India wanted railways to cross princely states for strategic and economic purposes it was prepared

A train of mixed single and two-tier stock on the Bombay Baroda and Central India Railway in 1876. The train is crossing the Narbada River on a temporary trestle bridge, the main bridge having been breached by floods. The breach is visible at the right of this photograph.

to offer assistance. The Nizam of Hyderabad, for instance, paid for the installation of his state railway but the Government undertook its construction and subsequent management. In 1863 the first narrow gauge locomotives in India were built for the Gaekwar of Baroda's railway although it was another ten years before they were in regular use. The Gaekwar had his own carriage sumptuously furnished in Indian style complete with a throne. Whenever he travelled by train – at least in the early days – he made one of his favourite court officials mount the engine as a precaution against accidents.

Emily Eden, the sister of Lord Auckland who was Governor-General from 1836 to 1842, had misgivings about the impact of the railways on the social structure she had known in India. 'Now that India has fallen under the curse of railroads', she lamented, 'and that life and property will soon become as insecure as they are here [in England], the splendour of a Governor-General's progress is at an end.' She predicted petulantly that 'the kootub will probably become a Railway Station . . . and the Governor-General will dwindle down into a first-class passenger with a carpet-bag.' Her fears were unfounded. The Viceroy and his Governors still continued to travel in a style that befitted their status. The first luxury carriage to be built in India was for the Governor of Bombay in 1863. Half of it was a combined sitting-room/bedroom and a dining room occupied the remaining space. A special train constructed by the East Indian Railway for the visit of the Prince of Wales in 1875 served as the viceregal train for about the next twenty-five years. The occasion of a further visit by the Prince and Princess of Wales in 1905 gave the East Indian Railway an opportunity to build another splendid train. It had nine saloon carriages, seven of them 72 feet long (about 12 feet longer than the carriages in use at that time in England). In addition to day and sleeping saloons, boudoir and dining saloon, it provided for the first time on Indian railways full-size baths with shower baths and douches.

Two viceregal trains were built in Edwardian times for the broad- and metre-gauge lines respectively. These long and immaculately white trains carried successive viceroys and their entourage on their official tours of the sub-continent, stopping at stations garlanded with flags and flowers and thronged with local dignitaries, patiently awaiting what for many of them would be the great event of their lives. Lord Curzon, who believed that ceremonial was a requisite manifestation of Britain's imperial role, deplored the sloppy arrangements to meet him on his arrival in Calcutta early in 1898. He wrote to Lord Hamilton, the Secretary of State for India:

SCINDIA STATE RAILWAY.

FARES.—First class, 1½ anna; second class, 9 pies; third class, 3 pies per mile.

WARDHA COAL STATE RAILWAY.

* The Junction of this Railway with the G. I. P. Railway is at Wardha, mileage 472 from Bombay. All passengers must change carriages at Wardha.

PATIALA RAILWAY.

From the Rajpura Junction Station on the Sind, Punjab and Delhi Railway.

Passengers can be booked through from stations on this line to all stations on the Sind Punjab and Delhi Railway (Punjab Section), Mooltan to Delhi inclusive.

A page from *Newman's Indian Bradshaw: a guide to travellers throughout India*, (Calcutta), January 1886. Each railway company published its own Indian A.B.C. guide and the *Indian Railway Travellers' Guide* provided the fullest information with good maps and railway routes for the whole of India. All Indian timetables used Madras time until Indian Standard Time was introduced in the twentieth century.

Prince of Wales' Saloon. This four-wheel saloon was built for the Prince of Wales to travel on the metre-gauge lines during his visit to India for the Durbar in 1876. It was constructed at Agra in 1875 and consists of an unpretentious saloon, minuscule toilet and shower and cramped sitting accommodation for attendants. Note the folding seats for attendants on the verandah. Strangely, this coach was never fitted with brakes. Three oil lamps, two in the saloon and one in the attendants' compartment, provided illumination. The engine is an 0-4-2 E-class which lost its tender and assumed a saddle-tank in 1913. Both are preserved at the Rail Transport Museum, Delhi.

In 1876, the Prince of Wales unconcernedly takes in the scenery from the footplate during an ascent from Colombo to Kandy. The Duke of Sutherland adopts a more prudent position as the engine sways round the curve at Sensation Rock. (*Graphic*, 1 May 1876.)

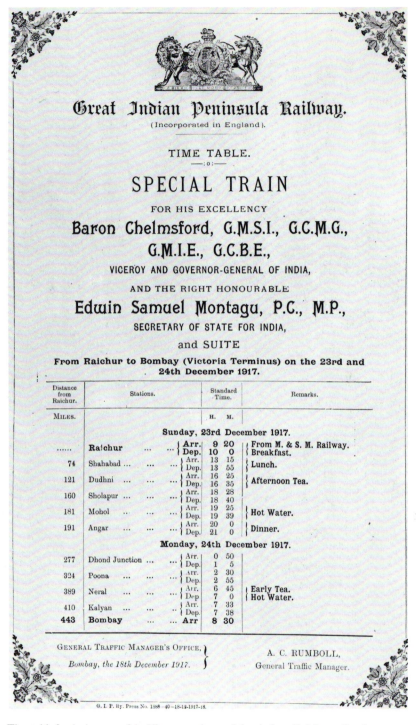

Great Indian Peninsula Railway.

(Incorporated in England).

TIME TABLE.

SPECIAL TRAIN

FOR HIS EXCELLENCY

Baron Chelmsford, G.M.S.I., G.C.M.G., G.M.I.E., G.C.B.E.,

VICEROY AND GOVERNOR-GENERAL OF INDIA,

AND THE RIGHT HONOURABLE

Edwin Samuel Montagu, P.C., M.P.,

SECRETARY OF STATE FOR INDIA,

and SUITE

From Raichur to Bombay (Victoria Terminus) on the 23rd and 24th December 1917.

Distance from Raichur.	Stations.		Standard Time.		Remarks.
MILES.			H.	M.	
	Sunday, 23rd December 1917.				
......	Raichur	Arr.	9	20	From M. & S. M. Railway.
		Dep.	10	0	Breakfast.
74	Shahabad	Arr.	13	15	Lunch.
		Dep.	13	55	
121	Dudhni	Arr.	16	25	Afternoon Tea.
		Dep.	16	35	
160	Sholapur	Arr.	18	28	
		Dep.	18	40	
181	Mohol	Arr.	19	25	Hot Water.
		Dep.	19	39	
191	Angar	Arr.	20	0	Dinner.
		Dep.	21	0	
	Monday, 24th December 1917.				
277	Dhond Junction	Arr.	0	50	
		Dep.	1	5	
324	Poona	Arr.	2	30	
		Dep.	2	55	
389	Neral	Arr.	6	45	Early Tea.
		Dep.	7	0	Hot Water.
410	Kalyan	Arr.	7	33	
		Dep.	7	38	
443	**Bombay**	**Arr.**	8	30	

GENERAL TRAFFIC MANAGER'S OFFICE,

Bombay, the 18th December 1917.

A. C. RUMBOLL,
General Traffic Manager.

G. I. P. Ry. Press No. 1888—40—18-12-1917-18.

Timetable for the journey of the Viceroy on the special train from Raichur to Bombay, 23–24 December 1917. The train stopped not only for meals but to distribute hot water.

The train drew up at the wrong place . . . The carpet was the size of a postage stamp. The band did not play God save the Queen. The Mil[itary] Sec[retary] forgot the names of most of the swells to whom he had to introduce me.

Although Curzon judged it a failure because it lacked the efficient organisation he expected of such occasions, one can be sure that for all the people, both European and Indian, gathered on the station on that memorable day it was an impressive display in which the emblazoned Viceregal train played an appropriate role, epitomising so aptly the British Raj, its power, its authority and its supreme confidence.

The railways of India commemorate not only departed British might but also the ingenuity and skill of its engineers and the foresight of men like Lord Dalhousie who, back in the 1850s, had urged the East India Company 'to engage in the introduction of a system of Railways into the Indian Empire' believing implicitly as he did in 'the vast and various benefits, political, commercial and social which that great measure of public improvement would unquestionably produce'.

Spectacular collision near Ludhiana on the North Western Railway on 27 December 1907. Two 4-4-0 M-class rear in a death embrace. Twenty people were killed and many injured. (*Illustrated London News*, 8 February 1908.)

Glossary

ABT Rack Principle   Where the gradient of a line was too steep (generally steeper than 1:20) to rely on the adhesion of plain wheels on rails, the ABT system was one of several adopted to ensure freedom from slipping. A toothed 'rack' rail was mounted between the running rails and a 'cog' wheel or wheels on the engine and train engaged this to provide increased traction and braking.

Atlantic   A name for locomotives with the 4-4-2 wheel arrangement.

Banking Engine   An engine designed and kept specifically for assisting trains up or down severe gradients.

Bogie Stock   Rolling stock mounted on a pair of (usually) four-wheel bogies pivoted to the frames so that they can swivel to accommodate curvature of the rails.

Classification of Locomotives   India followed British practice in adopting the Whyte notation which defines the wheel arrangement and number of wheels in each group, from front to back. The leading and trailing groups (if any) are described as carrying wheels which carry some of the weight and provide guidance; the middle group(s) are the driving wheels which provide the tractive force. Freight engines, with modest speed and high hauling power, have a higher proportion of driving to carrying wheels than express passenger engines which are designed for faster running with lighter loads.

Suffix letters denote the manner in which the water and fuel are carried. The absence of a suffix denotes a separate tender. Where the water and fuel are carried on the engine, in tanks and bunkers, the common suffix letters are:

T – Denoting side tanks each side of the boiler
ST – Denoting a saddle tank over the top of the boiler
Examples:
0-4-0 ST – An engine with no leading or trailing carrying wheels, four driving wheels (on two coupled axles) and water carried in a saddle tank over the boiler.
2-8-0   A freight or mixed-traffic engine with two leading carrying wheels, eight driving wheels on four coupled axles and no trailing carrying wheels. Water and fuel in separate tender.

Felloes   The sections, usually of wood, which form the rim of a built-up wheel.

Gauge   The distance between the inner faces of the two rails. The standards adopted for India were Broad gauge: 5ft 6in, Metre gauge: 1000mm (3ft 3⅜in), Narrow gauge: 2ft 6in and 2ft 0in.

Horse Gin   A machine in which a horse(s) was harnessed to an arm(s) attached to a vertical axle whereby, through gearing, it could operate a winch or other machinery.

Inside Cylinders   Cylinders mounted between the frames of the engine.

Journal   Bearing.

Link Motion   A form of mechanical linkage for operating the valves for admitting and exhausting steam to and from the cylinders and providing means for reversing the engine. Numerous variations on this theme were developed.

Nave   The centre, or hub, of a built-up wheel.

Outside Cylinders   Cylinders mounted outside the frames of the engine.

Outside Frames   Arrangement of main engine frames outside the driving wheels. This arrangement was popular on the narrower gauges to avoid crowding the frames and axle-boxes between the insides of the wheels.

Pacific   A name for locomotives with the 4-6-2 wheel arrangement.

Riggenbach compressive braking system   A method of using the engine cylinders to compress air as an aid to braking the train to reduce the wear on the normal train brakes on severe gradients.

13in x 20in cylinders   The first dimension denotes the bore, or diameter of the cylinder. The second dimension is the stroke of the piston.

Underframes   The main frames forming the basic structure on which is built the body of a wagon or carriage. Wood was used in early construction, soon superseded by iron and steel.

Walschaert's Valve Gear   A system of links for operating the cylinder valves which formed an alternative to the earlier link motion (*q.v.*). The Walschaert system became the virtual standard for main line locomotives in later years.

Reading list

Victor Bayley, *Permanent way through the Khyber*, London 1939
P. S. A. Berridge, *Couplings to the Khyber: the story of the North Western Railway*, Newton Abbot 1969
G. Davidson, *The railways of India: with an account of their rise, progress and construction, written with the aid of the Records of the India Office*, London 1868
M. A. Harrison, *Indian locomotives of yesteryear*, Bracknell 1972
H. Huddleston, *History of the East Indian Railway*, Calcutta 1926
Hugh Hughes, *Steam in India*, Truro 1976
Hugh Hughes, *Steam locomotives in India*, Parts I, II, III, Kenton 1977–80
N. Sanyal, *Development of Indian railways*, Calcutta 1930
J. N. Westwood, *Railways of India*, Newton Abbot 1974
Indian railways: one hundred years, Ministry of Railways, Government of India 1953
Railway Gazette, 28 May 1913, 12 November 1913, 17 September 1923

Plates

The first engine to enter Alwar on the Rajputana State Railway; Indian State Railways metre-gauge A-class 2-4-oT. This class was used mainly for construction purposes on new lines. One of these engines, Lord Lawrence is preserved at Gorakhpur. (*Graphic*, 26 December 1874.)

The first engine for the Peshawar Railway about to be floated across the Indus river at Attock on a raft consisting of three 'country' boats in the year 1881, for construction of the line to Peshawar and the Khyber Pass. The bridge across the river at Attock was opened in 1883. On the far bank the horse-gin and shaft stand as memorial to the abandoned attempt to tunnel the railway under the river. (*Graphic*, 28 January 1882.)

Bhore Ghat reversing station on the Great Indian Peninsula line from Bombay to Poona. The train is ascending the gradient (max. 1 :37) up the Western Ghats from Karjat. At the top right-hand corner it will reverse and proceed up the middle track in the opposite direction. The track on the left is the catch siding into which the points were set until downcoming trains had come to rest, when they were set for the train to proceed again down the main line. The catch siding was heavily graded up to the earth buffers to help bring runaway trains to rest. Note the banking engine on the rear of the train.

Disaster on the Bhore Ghat. On 25 January 1869 the mail train from Poona to Bombay ran away due to brake failure. The catch siding incline and earth buffer failed to arrest it and it crashed over the top of the embankment. Fourteen people died and many more were injured. The engine is one of the Kitson 0-8-0ST of 1866 (GIP 115), which was subsequently designated X Class, used to assist on the Ghat sections. (*Illustrated London News*, 6 March 1869.)

Dramatic engineering and dramatic scenery. Although Ceylon Railways were operated by the Colonial Office and were never part of the Indian railway system, they operated 5ft 6in and 2ft 6in gauge lines and had other features in common. The line from Colombo to Kandy rises to 1,690 feet, with much of the track bed hewn out of the rock-face and a drop of 1,000 feet over the edge. The line was opened in 1865.

East mouth of the Khojak tunnel at the extreme westerly end of the Kandahar State Railway (Chaman Extension Railway). The line was intended to reach Kandahar in Afghanistan, but never crossed the frontier, coming to a stop at Chaman, just beyond the far end of the tunnel. Note the functional aspect of the portal architecture, designed to provide defence against attack at either end.

The Khojak tunnel, started in 1888 and opened in 1891, is 12,870 feet long, and at that time was by far the longest in India. Much of it had to be driven through treacherous soft strata and this photograph (taken by Weightman, one of the engineers) shows the type of timbering employed. Notice the traditional dress of the Welsh miners, some sixty of whom brought experience from the building of the Severn Tunnel to the remote fastness of the North West Frontier.

Two intermediate shafts were sunk on the line of the tunnel to enable six headings to **be** driven simultaneously. This photograph shows the east shaft with its portable steam winch in the building for handling men and materials.

Access to the shafts from Sheelabagh, at the east mouth of the tunnel, was provided by a temporary rope-worked railway, designed by Weightman, involving gradients as steep as 1:2.5. Special trolleys were constructed to accept standard wagons on a level platform. In this photograph the level approach tracks are seen in the foreground, with the passing loop on the incline visible between the two trolleys, each loaded with a wagon. The rope haulage was operated by winches powered by locomotives and the trolleys counterbalanced each other.

Detail of the trolleys. Note the use of locomotive driving wheels at one end and tender wheels at the other, with inclined buffers. The trolley is at the top of the incline with the level approach track on the left.

Dapoorie Viaduct, linking Bombay Island with the mainland of Thana. Built by the
Great Indian Peninsula Railway in 1854 this bridge of twenty-two stone arches still
carries the main-line traffic.

Bridge spans were generally fabricated in Britain, dismantled after trial assembly and shipped out in pieces for transport to site where they would be assembled, stressed and riveted into final form before rolling into position. Here is such a span, manufactured by the Patent Shaft Axle Tree Company of Wednesbury, Staffordshire in 1886.

Final stages in the construction of the Curzon Bridge over the Ganges at Allahabad in 1905. The masonry piers founded on multiple wells and the silty nature of the soil are seen clearly. On the far side is the temporary construction railway which operated throughout the dry season. The locomotive is one of the Oudh and Rohilkund 0-6-0 B-class, of which No. 26 is preserved in the Rail Transport Museum in Delhi.

The Kullar Bridge built in 1899 on the Nilagiri Railway from Mettupalaiyam to Ootacamund shows the use of local stone for the piers and approaches with plate girder spans. The train is propelled uphill with the engine behind and the brakesman stands on the open platform of the leading coach. The engine is one of the 0-6-2T, S-class rack engines built by North British Locomotive Works in 1905.

The Kalka-Simla Railway was originally planned in 1903 with a gauge of 2ft oin, but strategic railways had by then adopted a gauge of 2ft 6in, so that re-gauging was necessary before the railway was opened. This bridge of local stone shows the use of a three-tier masonry arch construction reminiscent of Roman aqueducts. The engine is one of the 2-6-2T, K-class, built by the North British Locomotive Company, which were standard, with detail modifications, from 1905 throughout the life of steam on this line.

The Darjeeling-Himalayan Railway bridge across the Mahanaddy River in 1879 makes full use of timber from the local forests. The early third-class coaches with canvas screens provided good ventilation in the hot weather but scant protection from the cold and rain.

The bridge across the Gokteik Gorge at Hsipaw in Burma built in 1901 shows a break with tradition. The local limestone in the gorge was too friable to use for building purposes so a steel trestle design was adopted. The bridge is 2,260 feet long, 320 feet high and the track rises at a continuous 1:40 throughout its length. Design was undertaken by Sir Alexander Rendel & Sons and construction by the Pennsylvania Steel Company.

Testing a bridge at Bandi in Jaipur in 1916 after re-building. Two 0-6-0 F-class locomotives provide the load whilst the deflection of the centre span is measured with the aid of a wooden tripod.

Nature takes a hand. No sooner had the Manshahi River been bridged, in the State of
Cooch Behar, than the earthquake of 1897 caused this to happen. Floods and earthquakes
take a continuous toll of bridges and near-miracles of re-building are performed, using
standard bridge sections, held at strategic depots, and specially adapted cranes.

Wooden-bodied coaches under construction on mainly imported underframes and bogies at the Matunga Carriage Workshops in Bombay. Note the wagon body serving as the foreman's office.

Railway yard at Nagpur, western terminus of the Bengal-Nagpur Railway and junction with the Great Indian Peninsula Railway, *c.* 1910. Note the three-rail dual-gauge (2ft 6in and 5ft 6in) tracks, including the traverser. The locomotives on the left are 2ft 6in gauge and the stock on the right is 5ft 6in gauge. The locomotive on the left is 2-8-0 B-class no. 0047, built by the North British Locomotive Works in 1909 and probably just arrived. The small saddle-tank in the foreground is B.N.R. 176, *Locust*. This was one of six, built by Hunslet in 1869 for the 5ft 6in gauge Oudh & Rohilkund Railway. It was converted to 2ft 6in gauge at Kharagpur works in 1902 and sold to McLeod & Co. for the Bankura-Damoda River Railway in 1916.

Drawing Office
Iron Foundry. Pattern Shop.
Erecting Shop
Carpenter Shop
Erecting Shop
Workshop Supdt's Office.
Turning and Brass Finishing Shop

Railway Workshops at Jamalpur in 1897. Jamalpur was the first of the major railway towns,
built and administered by the railways and populated entirely by railway employees.

Unchanged since 1889, one of the indestructible 0-4-0 B-class tank engines of the Darjeeling-Himalayan Railway poses outside the railway workshops at Tindharia. The workshop is built on a spur of level ground and the main line climbs through 180° round the outside, with the road, to emerge at the right level on the left of the picture just before entering the station.

The tortuous nature of the Darjeeling-Himalayan Railway is well illustrated by this photograph during construction and before it was re-engulfed by the forest.

Village scene on the Darjeeling-Himalayan Railway. 0-4-0T A-class, No. 10 trundles its load through the village on its way down to the plains. This locomotive was built by Sharp Stewart in 1881 and was withdrawn by 1914. Note the prayer flags on the hillside.

After eighty-seven years of back-breaking toil, B-class No. 777 from the Darjeeling-Himalayan Railway takes its place with a four-wheel, third-class coach in the Rail Transport Museum, Delhi. Built in 1889 by Sharp, Stewart, this is the oldest survivor of its class and is still in full working order.

Steam railcars were used by several railways for minor passenger services. In 1907, Nasmyth, Wilson supplied five railmotors to the East Indian Railway. These were saloons mounted on one powered and one trailing bogie. In 1925, the saloons were scrapped, but the power bogies were rebuilt at Jamalpur as shunting engines. *Hercules* and *Phoenix* survived at Jamalpur and the Rail Transport Museum, Delhi, respectively; *Sampson* and *Ajax* went for scrap, but *Atlas* was sold to Calcutta Corporation to work the refuse line from Entally until he, too, joined *Sampson* and *Ajax* in oblivion.

Ramgotty Mukerjee was the last General Manager of the 4ft 0in gauge Nalhati-Azimgunge Light Railway, built in 1862. The railway was taken over by the East Indian Railway and re-gauged to 5ft 6in in 1892. *Ramgotty* was re-gauged to 5ft 6in and became a shunting engine at Jamalpur until sold to Calcutta Corporation for refuse hauling in 1951. In his centenary year, *Ramgotty* expired, but in 1974, he was rescued, returned to Jamalpur and now reposes in the Rail Transport Museum in Delhi. It is the only locomotive extant in India with outside Gooch valve gear, and was built by Ajubault of Paris in 1862.

In 1907, the Patiala State Monorail Trainway purchased four extraordinary 0-3-0T locomotives with outriggers to operate the line from Patiala towards Sunam. They finished work in 1914, but this one is now preserved and working at the Rail Transport Museum in Delhi. Coupled to it is a re-built saloon which was once the inspection saloon for Colonel Bowles, the builder of the railway.

The second attempt to build a line up to Quetta involved a temporary section laid with metre-gauge track instead of 5ft 6in, between Hirok and Kolpur in the Bolan Pass. This was heavily graded (1:23) with curves of 200 feet radius. To work this section, double Fairlie locomotives were employed with rolling stock adapted to carry broad-gauge wagons through the section. The route was re-aligned and converted to broad gauge some two years later and four of the double Fairlie locomotives ended their life working on the Nilagiri Railway.

Animal power has always been readily available in India. Two elephants are engaged in a shunting operation at a mill on the Bengal-Nagpur Railway.

Elephants captured in the Mysore Khedda in 1895 are entrained on the Madras Railway
on the first stage of journeys to new working locations.

Loading camels into railway wagons.

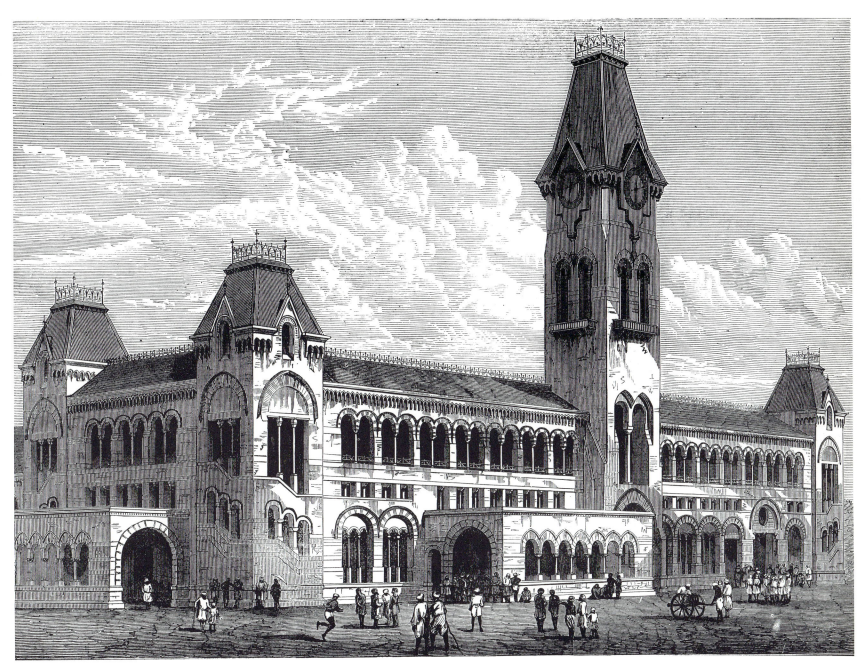

Madras Central Station, 1868; 'all ornamentation should be avoided'.

Lahore Station. One of the best examples of the fortified stations erected shortly after the
Indian Mutiny, 1857.

Lucknow Station as rebuilt in 1926 with dominant Islamic features in keeping with its environment.

Nawab Station, typical of the single platform station with overall roof to be found in the
Lucknow-Agra area.

Howrah Station, Calcutta terminus of the East Indian Railway, as re-built in red brick
in 1906. This is the largest passenger terminal in India. (*Indian State Railways Magazine*,
XI:7, 30 April 1938.)

Some stations assumed a grandeur which bore little relation to their importance. The humble metre-gauge station at Junagad is hidden behind the imposing station clock tower and façade at Reay Gate.

JUNAGUD STATION.

English in name if not surroundings. Adderley Station on the Nilagiri Railway on the steep (1:12.28) rack section of the line. The rack can be seen at the two approaches, but is omitted through the short level section within station limits. Typically English names such as Hillgrove, Runnymede, Wellington and Lovedale remind one of an English presence as they mingle with Mettupalaiyam, Coonoor, Aravankadu, Ketti and Ootacamund.

Third-class waiting room at Kharagpur. An empty hall, with water laid on outside.

The classical portico of the Bengal-Nagpur Railway Agent's residence proclaimed the status of its occupant. Railway employees were allocated accommodation commensurate with their rank.

A district engineer's home at Tandur, designed by Alexander Izat, but trimmed at the time of building to reduce cost. It covered 2,567 sq ft and cost £770. Functionalism is the keynote.

An assistant engineer's bungalow at Hinganmalli. E. H. Stone in *The Nizam's State Railway* 1876 writes: '. . . a glance at Jack or Tom as he is. His work which is hard and troublesome lasts all day long and his dress and personal appearance accommodate themselves to the circumstances of his position. His nearest neighbour lives 12 miles off, across a country with no roads. His house and immediate surroundings you see in the photograph; and as for future honour and promotion, he has been studying the "Classified List" lately, and finds that, with hard work and fair luck, he will probably be a Chief Engineer in the space of 129 years.'

A railway foreman's bungalow at the Kharagpur workshops of the Bengal-Nagpur
Railway. An imposing edifice for an important man.

Staff quarters, Indian type B, at Kharagpur Workshops of the Bengal-Nagpur Railway.

Dining room of the apprentices' boarding house at Kharagpur. Polished teak and silver
plated cruet sets provide a suitable setting for sporting trophies.

European Institute at Kharagpur. The band of the Railway Volunteers would play from the bandstand, ladies would take tea and gossip on the lawn and the billiards and card tables would provide recreation after dark. The atmosphere would be as English as the climate permitted.

Guards' and drivers' quarters at Chaman military outpost at the end of the line; three
miles away was the frontier with Afghanistan.

The Railway Institute at Quetta in the 1880s.

Patiala Station. A fine example of the re-use of materials. The canopy supports are rolled out of used railway line and the fret infill is of local cast iron. Such structures were common and frequently displayed an elegance combined with functional simplicity which contrasted with the ornate decoration of façades and towers.

Drinking water arrangements for lower class passengers.

At many of the large river crossings, where bridges had not been built the railways operated their own ferries. In some cases, the passengers and goods were detrained on one bank and ferried to a railhead on the other side. In other cases, train ferries were provided onto which the rolling stock could be placed.

The railways had to be prepared to support the armed forces at short notice. Here is a narrow (2ft 6in) gauge motor ambulance built at Kharagpur. Note the inevitable bulb horn on the driver's platform.

Municipal authorities employed railways, broad- or narrow-gauge, to remove garbage and night-soil to tips. Not surprisingly, they came to be known as the 'stink expresses', though they must have been the slowest expresses in the land. Here, narrow-gauge Orenstein and

Koppel No. 810 goes about its unsavoury task in the streets of Jodhpur. Note the bell which clanged continuously on its flexible stalk to herald its approach.

March 1907. The inaugural train climbs the hill from Neral Junction to Matheran on the 2ft oin gauge Matheran Light Railway. The engine, a 0-6-0 articulated tank, was one of four built by Orenstein and Koppel on the principle evolved by Sir Arthur Haywood of Duffield Bank, Derbyshire in 1879. All four engines were still at work on this line in 1979. The rather spartan accommodation for passengers did eventually yield to the introduction of closed but basic coaches.

Typical first-class accommodation in corridor stock on bogie underframes in 1908. The windows had shutters which could be raised so that the windows could be opened to increase ventilation without jeopardising security. Note the provision of electric lights and fans.

English brocade and ornate brass fittings provide the finishing touches to the finest Indian craftsmanship in this luxurious private saloon. Most of the Native Princes had their own private saloons, or trains; this was built for the Maharaja of Benares.

Third class travelled hard. Slatted wooden seats arranged back-to-back in three tiers provided seating, squatting or lying space. Electric lighting is replacing earlier gas and oil lamp fittings. The black panels above the windows are ventilators covered on the outside by sunshades. Fans have yet to appear, but the clerestory roof contributed slightly to headroom and ventilation. Note the lamp bowl with its accumulation of roasted greenfly!

Lady Curzon's special train effects a short halt, probably for the distribution of hot water, in Hyderabad in 1902. The locomotive is one of the 4-6-0 A-class of the Nizam's Guaranteed State Railways, one of which is preserved in the Rail Transport Museum in Delhi.

Guests arriving at Gwalior Station on the occasion of the visit of T.R.H. The Prince and
Princess of Wales to the Maharaja Scindia in 1905.

The Maharaja Scindia of Gwalior developed an extensive narrow (2ft 0in) gauge network of railways in his State. From the station, a spur ran to the palace, with his private saloons and engine. When the engine finally expired, he built a mausoleum for it in the palace grounds, where, somewhat incomplete, it stands to this day. This photograph taken in 1918 shows his train against the palace wall with a later engine.

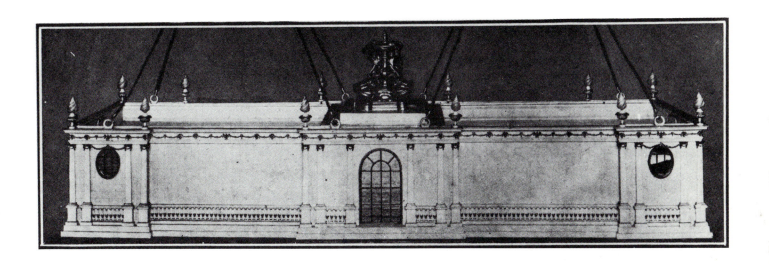

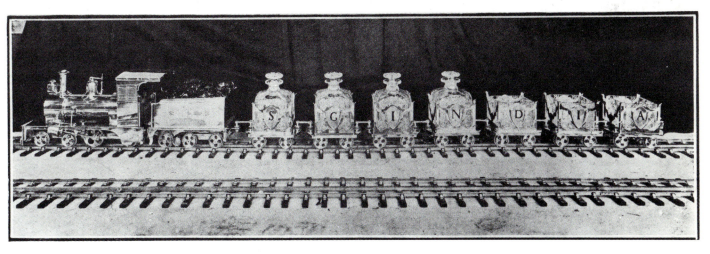

Railways became not only essential, but fashionable. The banqueting table in the Palace
at Gwalior had a centrepiece of silver which, at the touch of a button, rose to reveal the
silver model train which then circulated the liqueurs and cigars to the guests.
(*Illustrated London News*, 20 January 1906.)

H.R.H. the Princess of Wales' day saloon of the Royal train specially designed and constructed at the Lillooah Carriage Works of the East Indian Railway for the Royal visit in 1905. (Johnston & Hoffman's *Royal Tour Souvenir Album India 1905–6*, Calcutta 1906.)

The bedroom of H.R.H. The Princess of Wales in the Royal train. (*Royal Tour Souvenir Album.*)

Bengal-Nagpur Railway 4-6-0 G.S. class locomotive *Duke of Connaught*, used on Royal trains.

782347